THE
CHURCH
RECLAIMS
THE
CITY

by Paul Moore, Jr.

Foreword by Dr. Marshal L. Scott

THE SEABURY PRESS
NEW YORK • 1964

Acknowledgments

Grateful acknowledgment is made to the following publishers for permission to use copyrighted material from the titles listed:

Collier Books—Max Weber, *The City*

Wm. B. Eerdmans Publishing Co.—William Stringfellow, *A Private and Public Faith*

Doubleday & Company, Inc.—Gibson Winter, *The Suburban Captivity of the Church*, copyright © 1961 by Gibson Winter

Harcourt, Brace & World, Inc.—Lewis Mumford, *The City in History*

For Honor, Paul, Adelia, Rosemary, George,
Marian, Daniel, Susanna, and Patience

Foreword

It is now common knowledge that there is a population explosion on earth but it is not so widely understood that there is also a population tide—toward the cities.

As the world-wide flow of peoples draws mankind from the land into urban places there is economic, social, and political disruption of old cultures and new cultural patterns are emerging. Sometimes the trends are fairly clear; at other times there is only confusion.

Most of the time sociologists can describe what is happening but there is little that they can do to shape events. They can observe but they do not participate, ordinarily. This is a valid, but limited, contribution to the common welfare.

Churchmen are involved, and they do participate. But they do not always understand what is happening. And when they do understand they often feel helpless before the forces pressing down upon them.

The spreading blight of "inner-city" relentlessly pushes outward into "middle-city," even into the older suburbs. Congregations keep fleeing toward the newer and more comfortable outer circles. New and "different" folk flow in behind them. A Christian ministry among the American white middle classes is not necessarily easy but it produces evidences of fruitfulness and "successful" parishes can be maintained for a time (usually a generation or two) until the neighborhood changes. But in the older central city the going is rough. Even when renewal replaces blight the church does not find its ministry much easier. For the new people of rebuilt neighborhoods are usually in the public housing projects or high-rise middle and upper-class apartment houses, neither of which is fertile territory for the traditional parish church.

Across the years there have been concerned churchmen and dedicated clergymen and laymen who have given their lives to Christian ministry in the more difficult sections of cities.

Some years ago extensive sociological studies were made of city churches and in this decade a rash of books have been published on the city church. Most of these have been variations on the sociology of religion.

This new book by Paul Moore is different.

It begins where most of the books leave off. It could not have been written this way if the other studies had not been made and it reflects and builds upon the others. Rather than repeating or restating the analysis, it proposes some things that can be done. Yet it is not a mere "how-to-do-it-kit" although it treats many practical matters.

The focus here is on a biblical, theological, historical church in the modern world. This keeps the horse before the cart (a somewhat out-moded figure).

The authenticity of this book lies in its author. He is no ordinary person and his is no ordinary experience. He comes from a family of great prominence in American industry. He could have held positions of responsibility in the business world. Or, he could have gone to "important" parishes. Instead, he and his remarkable wife chose to go, along with two colleagues, into the most difficult parish that several eastern bishops could find for them. They poured their lives into the lives of men, women, and children of the crowded slums of Jersey City. They brought

Christ and his redemption to the people from whom the church had run away. In fact, the first thing they did was to tear down the "Keep Out" sign, that hung on the iron fence outside the church.

This is not an armchair study. Paul Moore is a man of unusual intelligence, of vigorous and disciplined faith, and he has the poise, humor, and realism of one who has been there. He lived the ministry about which he writes. He speaks as one having authority.

The chapter by Mrs. Moore on the clergyman's family in the inner-city is worth the price of the book, whatever price tag the publishers put on it.

MARSHAL L. SCOTT

Table of Contents

Preface

"*The glory is the thing happening; it is not, though in our talk we seem to make it so and can only believe in it so, an accident of the thing happening. The glory of God is in facts. The almost incredible nature of things is that there is no fact which is not in His glory. This is the great inclusion which makes the City. If, to use terms of space, we ascend towards it, it is still that which descends out of heaven, and is the cause and course of our ascent. The language of it is in the great interchange of fiery tongues by which the Spirit manifested at the beginning.*"

—CHARLES WILLIAMS

HUNDREDS of Christians are faced with a nagging problem today in America—and throughout the world. They see the modern city in all its overwhelming size and power sweeping human life along unwanted ways, crushing sensitive human hearts, and tearing frail loves apart. And they see the Church seeming powerless to resist, to guide, or to change. A priest kneels before the altar and is filled with a vision of the heavenly Jerusalem, but before long his thoughts are torn away by the rush of traffic at the Church's door. And this is more, much more, than a nagging problem for the individual Christian: it has come to symbolize the life struggle and (sometimes we fear) the death struggle of Christianity as we know it against principalities which are determining our way of life. These principalities are not subject to direct attack, nor can they be exorcised.

The Church has been a long time recognizing this struggle for what it is. A few prophetic voices cried out many years ago, but it is only in the years since the end of World War II that a school of thought has been developing and plans of action forged to resist the wave of destruction. These thoughts, plans, and actions have been gathered together in various books and articles, as can be seen in the bibliography at the back of this book. These books have been of two principal kinds. One group has dealt with the culture as a whole and its relation to the Christian faith; theologians like William Temple, Reinhold Niebuhr, and Paul Tillich have dug deeply into their implications for our day. Sociologists have revealed the dynamics of disintegrating parishes and secularized churchmen. The most recent and helpful of these efforts is Gibson Winter's book, *The Suburban Captivity of the Church*. Psychologists are dealing with the impact of their discipline upon the individual Christian and the culture in which he finds himself.

The other kind of book is the anecdotal description of various successful efforts of the city church. Paul Musselman's *The Church on the Urban Frontier* covers the subject well for the Episcopalians; Ross Sanderson's *The Church Serves the Changing City* covers a broader scope. There is something of a vacuum, however, in the area of practical handbooks useful to the interested layman, seminarian, or clergyman who is unfamiliar with the field. Murray H. Leiffer's *The Effective City Church* is most helpful and covers every aspect of urban church life. It does not attempt, however, to enter into the problems within the soul of the Church, nor does it attempt to speak to the liturgical Church.

This book, then, will be a handbook on urban work. I find, in going about the country, great eagerness on the part of the Church to *do* something and at the same time an unnecessary ignorance about some of the things which can be done and have been done. Deep solutions to the civilization in which we are engulfed as articulated in the metropolis are still far from us, but in the meantime there are works to be done, souls to be saved, and the Kingdom to fight for. The long-prayed-for solutions will only come to a Church which is involved and torn in the struggle.

1. Inner-City Battleline

"Hell, like heaven, has many mansions."

—CHARLES WILLIAMS

THE modern city has movement, vigor, purposiveness, power—and often beauty, too. From the vantage point of a skyscraper tower one is held entranced by the seemingly miraculous ebb and flow of life along its arteries, the unexpected rhythms of its skyline, the sharp contrasts of pattern it exhibits, its monumental statement of vigor and dynamism.

Stand, at noon hour, on the steps of New York's Trinity Church, Wall Street, and watch the thousands of passers-by hurrying back and forth to lunch. Steps are springy; faces tensed toward goals. And although the goals may not always be right, and the faces sometimes too tense, there is sureness, nonetheless. The towers that gloom overhead do not intimidate these passers-by. Each of them has his place inside one of these towers—a small desk with a picture of his children, a coffeepot and a friend, or perhaps a large office suite with hunting prints on the wall, and on the desk a scale model of "our" latest product. These are man's towers; he has built them and made them places of his power.

Here is a world-center of decision, where men's minds and wills relentlessly work, creating movements, switching courses of action, choosing new directions for undertakings, with changes resulting here—abroad—in Asia. Strategy is carefully evaluated by a board of directors in one tower, and by a union executive committee in its own tower a block away.

Here at the center of power, in most cities, is often a church. Its influence should not be overestimated, but it *is* here. Some stop to enter its silence for a moment of what they call peace, or for a strengthening of resolution, or to utter a desperate cry for help. They are directed, perhaps driven, by outside forces of all kinds, yet they retain some space of freedom into which the voice of the Spirit of God can speak. (And that voice would speak more clearly if some of God's people knew better how to pray and others listen.) The Church belongs here at the center of the city and its presence should be more effective, for usually it goes to the board meetings, only as a silent, unknown, invisible watcher within each man.

The center of the city is also a place of lonely homelessness; of bitter loneliness such as that of the white collar worker pictured in *The Apartment*, who is only a number behind a desk. The movie shows him to be a pawn in the hands of management, one who simply goes home at night to his rooming house, his television set, and his TV supper. When he has to stand outside in the snow, while his boss uses his apartment for a date, his stature and dignity as a person is finally lost completely.

This grim story is also, in one way or another, that of many employed downtown, for our culture is one that throws off their employees as soon as their work is done, providing no way of life, no home, no folkways, no community, no real friends, no one who cares much what happens.

Nor are those who manage the great downtown complex always better off. They can buy surroundings of pleasure; many of them do have homes and families in the fullest sense. Yet they, too, are not without loneliness, aimlessness. Some are deeply opposed to the policies of the corporations for which they work; some are forced to make the very decisions of which they disapprove. Some feel guilty about decisions they cannot avoid or not guilty enough about those they can. Owing either to the anomaly of the life they are leading or to the combination of tracklessness, manic speed, and movement which the culture produces, theirs is a hard-won equilibrium. A healthy family life is maintained only through great effort. These men are not just ambitious; they are driven, caught, running a treadmill with no control over its direction. Theirs can be a lonely life, often a life with a tragic end.

CREATIVITY—AND HUMAN FRUSTRATION

The downtown power-center is a strange mixture of creativity and human frustration. To each of these aspects the Church owes a ministry—a ministry of guidance, of love, and of understanding.

All of downtown, however, is not made up of desks and people sitting behind them. There are packages to be delivered, meals to be cooked, wastebaskets to be emptied, and all the people to do these jobs. At night thousands of workers appear, to scrub and clean, to straighten and wash. The Church has a ministry to these people, too. Yet they do not even dream that the well-appointed downtown church is there for them, the symbol of the poor man who died for them on the Cross, unless, that is, some combination of odd chance or supreme effort on the part of the Church has reached their lives.

There are others downtown besides those who work there. There are those, for example, who are drawn to Times Square, the Loop, or the Bowery as though by an invisible magnet of anonymity, the flotsam and jetsam of humanity. When, at any level of society, a person is cut loose from his ties, sooner or later he will be found floating downtown. He may take a room at a club while his wife sues him for divorce. Or he may stay at the Salvation Army if he can't afford something better, or he may even spend the night in a doorway because the Salvation Army has no room or perhaps knows him too well.

Another section of downtown is the so-called entertainment or theater district—the Times Square district. It is early evening when we arrive there and we saunter into a small, colorless bar, so dark that it is difficult to see anything at first. We find our way to the bar, where all conversation immediately stops. Gradually we begin to see ourselves reflected in the blue mirror behind the bottles of rare liqueur that nobody ever drinks.

Turning around, we make out what the darkness has been hiding—a row of cheerless booths in imitation red leather. In one, a couple is talking in anger. At another, a blonde displays herself, scarcely hiding her motive. From a third two young men peer out with wandering eyes; one of them will soon rise to go to the bar when a single, well-dressed man enters. Suddenly a healthy, noisy group of college kids burst in; the place shudders and the occupants withdraw within themselves, as if such good times, such joy, had no business here. The collegians do not stay long.

For some this area is a recreation area, but it is also the place where the unhappy and the socially unacceptable gather. Here are found the totally rejected, as well as those who are driven to let some unacceptable part of themselves out into the air once in a while. To the needs of these people the downtown underworld ministers: the bartenders, the cab drivers who will recommend an illegal spot, the dance-hall girls, the prostitutes, male and female for male or female, depending upon which socially unacceptable drive compels the seeker. Here are the narcotics peddlers, the after-hour bars, the hotels that ask no questions.

The underworld ministers have circles of their own, complete with structure and language, and a series of subcultures: the alcoholic world, the narcotic world, the dance-hall world, the burlesque world, the homosexual world, the call-girl world.

The Church is here, too. Very occasionally someone seeks it out, and happy is he if there is a priest who knows his world and can talk to him in his own language without being shocked.

Clustered around the downtown nucleus are the other parts of the inner city—the waterfront, for example, where one can see great cargo nets swinging in the air, and the glistening backs of the men guiding them down the hold. There is a health and power here. Don't be afraid of the loud shouts, the cussing, the banging of iron, or the dirty clothes. As we move along the docks great, coarse, powerful smells, accompanied by great, coarse, powerful noises assault us. There is something romantic about the sea and its power to draw people to it, giving to even the worst of lives a stature and dimension never found amid the niceties of white-collardom. No wonder the priest-workers of Marseilles were drawn to the docks as a place to begin their work!

Industry is, to some extent, leaving the city, but it will be a long time before any city is without it. The docks, the garment district, leather shops, candy factories, can companies, great roaring steel mills, all of which are little cities in themselves, are still to be found in the city.

In these areas and districts anything which could be described as a church is rarely present. The Church is seldom there even in the mind of the worker on his job. No decisions are generally required of him (except perhaps the decision to stay or leave); he leads a life of putting in time. Yet, strangely enough, he is joined by the most direct economic ties to the downtown financial area. His life may be very different from that of his white-collared, well-tailored "brother" at the tables of decision, but more than anyone else he affects them and is affected by them. The Church does not have to be absent, for when it is involved naturally in an industrial situation, it does have something to say, as the motion picture *On the Waterfront* demonstrated rather melodramatically.

In another direction, but also close to the downtown core we reach the high-rise apartment area. (In New York City this area is a little farther away—along Park Avenue, Fifth Avenue, and Central Park West.) These apartments are occupied, for the most part, by downtown executives, young couples who haven't yet moved to the suburbs, and returnees—that is, older couples, who have raised their families and are now back in the city.

These older couples who have returned are coming to be an ever larger percentage of the urban population. Behind their return to the city, in many cases, was the hope of living comfortably in their declining years near places of interest. That hope has rarely been fulfilled. While some may saunter down the street in leisurely fashion, more often they hurry by so that no one will guess that they really have no particular destination. Some will talk to a mere stranger with the greatest enthusiasm; others never talk to anyone at all. Most of them, however, live in quiet desperation, terrorized by mounting medical bills or worrying over creeping cancer. Then the husband or wife falls sick, and his mate will nurse him in hate—torn with anger that he or she must spend his last energies on one he ceased to love long ago. Or perhaps, one will nurse the other in love—torn with grief to see his loved one fade away while he is powerless to help.

But on the whole these are fashionable apartments with the familiar well-uniformed doorman, the new awning with polished brass poles, the chic woman briskly walking her miniature poodle at the curb. As we continue we pass rows of brownstones. There are small but clear signs that they are still well-tended, signs which give tone to the whole area: a new doormat, freshly painted window frames, glistening dark green flower pots, a glimpse of a white-walled interior and the corner of a contemporary painting.

We are still "uptown" in the area where the Church can carry on with a traditional program, dealing with people accustomed to a traditional church, people who expect to go every Sunday morning to the same sort of place they have attended all their lives—a handsome, comfortable church which gives guidance and can be used in times of crisis. This is the kind of church they want and have, and some of them spend a good deal of time there listening to lectures, attending Bible classes, and doing good works of one kind or another. For some of them the Church even may have become the very center of their lives; within its leisured pace they may have found, after some searching, God.

We are quickly out of this neighborhood, as we shall notice by the different small shops we pass. And the houses, even though of the same brownstone and located within a hundred yards of their well-kept twins, are different. Right away one can sense the change. There are no signs of good grooming; the brownstone is flaking and window paint is peeling; a sign is hung out—"ROOMS." Right here, over the edge of the core of every city, lies an urban section called by sociologists the "blighted area," and proof positive that economics and social forces are the determining factors in the way people live in the city.

As we continue along such a street, the change is even more violent; within a block or so we are surrounded by hundreds of ragged children. Above us the windows are open and women are leaning out, resting their elbows on a pillow, to watch the street below. We are now in what used to be called the slums. The view is the same whether it be here, down in the Lower East Side tenements, up in Spanish Harlem, over in Jersey City,

or Brooklyn; whether the city be Chicago, Indianapolis, or San
Francisco. Whether the inhabitants be "poor white," Negro,
Puerto Rican, or Mexican, the life is the same. It centers around
money to pay the bills, fighting the landlord and bullying him
into fixing the gas line or the plumbing, keeping the children—
or oneself—out of trouble. Here we shall meet the short-order
cook from Wall Street or the dock worker on his way home.

Here and there in the area the blight may be relieved by huge
public-housing developments, like those on New York's Lower
East Side, built to accommodate specific economic groups. In
them one can see exaggerated the tendencies of whatever group
inhabits them—more children, more baby carriages, more teen-
agers with more duck-tail haircuts. Often it seems (although
this may be a subjective impression) that something is missing
in these housing projects—that in the cleanup the life-germ was
sterilized too.

Beyond these slums are more rooming houses, then slightly
better apartment buildings, and, finally, the so-called transition
areas, where the population is changing rapidly from one social
group to another and the housing is changing accordingly. One-
family houses become two- or three-family houses. In other cases
the run-down old houses are picked up, brushed off, and cleaned
up by their new owners. This, however, is the exception; usually
the real estate men and the landlords use the old houses to the
limit without repair or maintenance. There is often a quick turn-
over in ownership; and as the street becomes dilapidated, the
blight spreads.

Beyond the transition areas lie the suburbs of the white-collar
worker—Astoria, Queens, and the Upper Bronx—and beyond
them the suburbs of abundance in ring after ring of an ever-
ascending economic scale.[1]

[1] See Jane Jacobs, *The Death and Life of American Cities* (New York:
Random House, 1961) for a detailed description of the city.

DYNAMIC MOVEMENT

Any picture of the city is necessarily a static one, but the city itself is far from static. If any one characteristic is essential to an understanding of urban life, it is movement. There is movement from home to work, exurbia to executive suite, tenement to dock. There are both long moves and short moves. There is movement up the economic scale. House and neighborhood are symbols of one's place in life, like caste signs on the forehead; as one's station changes, so must one's neighborhood. An alert pastor knows that the good news of the promotion of one of his parishioners will also mean the bad news of his moving out of the parish to a "better" neighborhood. Age brings people back to the inner city and the arrival of children sends out those who can afford to go. A broken home means return to the inner city for the man and sometimes the woman, a return for a time to lick wounds or to seek another mate; being single is less lonely here than in family-centered suburbia.

There is movement due to other more complex causes. A ghetto in the inner city becomes so full that it literally bursts its seams; the members of the ghetto are "allowed" by some mysterious (or not so mysterious) consensus to "invade" a neighborhood. Behind this movement is a long series of cause and effect. The rural South can support fewer and fewer persons. Jobless Southerners move to the city to look for work; they swell the ghetto. The ghetto's top layer moves out to a newly integrated neighborhood. The former residents of the latter move out further or, if they are elderly, go back to the high-rise inner city.

So it goes; the pot is continually being stirred by economic and social forces. A decision made in a New York bank's board room, an unwritten agreement between realtors, the invention of a new piece of automotive equipment, tension in Berlin—these and hundreds of other seemingly unrelated factors affect the movement and change of the city. Welfare agencies, recreation groups, churches, real-estate lobbies, even city planners and others concerned in city government may attempt to channel these forces into less destructive paths, but their efforts are usually defensive and often too weak to buck the economic pressure. The Church must recognize this mobility and be prepared to coordinate her ministry to meet it.

Moreover, each parish church within its own socio-economic area has its own specific problems, although all share the common problem of population mobility. And the failure to meet that problem lies behind the great urban shut-down of the churches in the last fifty years.

Each parish church also has its own particular strengths and weaknesses. No one parish, however, will have a comprehensive inner-city ministry. For the urban problem must be met by a body of broader organizational scope—that is, the diocese, district, or presbytery.

And while the suburbs are a part of that city, the ministry to the suburbs is generally in no need of propaganda. The part of suburban ministry which is weakest is that which concerns the work and social responsibility of its members. The inner city is the symbol of these concerns, the listening post for problems in these areas. Thus the ministry to the suburbs will also greatly benefit from an emphasis on the problems of the inner city.

In other ages and other places the/focal point of the Church's program may have been the countryside or the town, but in this age and nation the focal point must be the inner city. It is there that the social ills of our society are most evident. It is there that the ministry of pastoral love is most desperately needed, and it is there that the decisions are made which affect the society in which we live. Yet it is the inner city which is the most neglected missionary front in our country today!

For this reason, this book will address itself particularly to the problems of the inner city.

2. The Two Cities

"The Kingdom—or, apocalyptically, the City—is the state into which Christendom is called; but, except in vision, she is not yet the City. The City is the state which the Church is to become."

—CHARLES WILLIAMS

THE Church can never be separated from history, nor can any problem facing the Church be understood without looking at her heritage. This chapter will attempt to touch upon some of the ideas and movements of the past which have a direct bearing upon the Church as she confronts the city today.

Jesus grew up in a village; his roots were in an agricultural society. His images, his thought patterns, and his way of life were rural. He preached to farmers, shepherds, and fishermen. However, as resistance to his preaching and healing ministry grew, it became clear that the heart of the resistance lay within the power structure of his society and that this structure was based in Jerusalem. The turning point in his life came when he said, "Behold, I go to Jerusalem." Peter's confession, "Thou art the Christ," and his own realization on the Mount of Transfiguration of his peculiar unity with the Father surrounded this critical moment. In other words, as soon as his Messianic vocation was clearly understood by Jesus and discovered by his disciples, he was impelled to confront the heart of his society. This was to be found then, as it is found today, in the city.

The idea of the city was already highly developed in Judaism; the city as glory and the city as evil each held its sway over the Jewish soul. The cities of the plain, Sodom and Gomorrah, in the dim reaches of prehistory, represented perversion of love and demonic self-centeredness. The cities of the Philistines stood for idolatry and materialism; Babylon was the symbol of exile and defeat. Only Jerusalem spelled glory. There was the tabernacle of the Holy of Holies, the final resting place of the Ark; and around her image flowed the history and destiny of the Jews. Jerusalem not only contained their life but symbolized the rise and fall of the Chosen People. The state of Jerusalem showed forth the favor or rejection of Jahweh. To this city the people came on pilgrimage and holiday; thus it represented holiness, history, festivity, and joy. It drew with power the spirit of the Jewish nation.

To this place Jesus came and over the vanity of this place Jesus wept. Into its center he drove his love and with its decaying leadership he battled to the death. That death was his victory; although it seemed the victory of the city, it became her death.

Thus Jerusalem became a deepened symbol to the Christian community, and a resultant ambivalence to the city was set deep in the Christian soul. Jerusalem had slain her Saviour, and yet the purpose of his death was the founding of the Jerusalem which is above, the heavenly Jerusalem. Toward this Eschaton the Church has been drawn with power all through her history. As the glistening ancient city dwelt upon a mountaintop over the life of the Chosen People, so the glorified image of the City dwells eternally over the society of the Church. As the history of the Jews ebbed and flowed through those narrow streets of

Sion, so has the history of the Church risen and fallen with her
relation to the cities of the world.

It is well known that although Jesus was a countryman, and
although the gospel first was preached in rural Galilee, his followers spread the news of his salvation through the cities of the
Roman empire. To the several kinds of cities of that empire the
New Testament authors reacted in a variety of ways. Paul chal-
lenged the emptiness of the Greek city, the *polis*, which had
passed its prime as a way of life; he inveighed against the dis-
solute life of the seaport town of Corinth. He met the commer-
cialized religion of the cult-city of Ephesus head-on, and yet he
gloried in his own Roman citizenship. In I Peter the author accepts with docility the imperium of Rome and relies upon the
Pax Romana, the ordered society within which the Church was
growing. In Revelation, on the other hand, under the heat of
the persecutions, Rome becomes Babylon and the City the
symbol of the Kingdom of God. One looks in vain for a uniform
biblical view of the city; each view expressed varies with the
author and the context of his expression. This variety in itself
has something to say—that the city as a unit of human society
is basically neutral. Its virtue and its vice depend upon the purpose toward which the city presses and the quality of the relationships within its walls.

New Testament Christians were realistic about the cities in
which they preached. They accepted urban living as a fact. Nowhere is there to be found any tendency to move away from the
city, to go back to the farm. They were not afraid of the city as
an entity and did not castigate it as a human institution. They
did not belabor the problems of the inner city and the suburbs,
but they went about their business preaching the gospel to anyone who would listen. The Christian community, at least in the
beginning, was so filled with the Spirit that all who embraced
this new way of life let go the differences of their earthly situa-

tions. They associated as equals in the new Jerusalem, in the Eucharistic fellowship.

POST-BIBLICAL CITIES

Post-biblical history shows the Church living within the social order and, for the most part, respecting its protection, even though at times persecutions arose and the Church rebelled against the corruptions of the secular life around her. Later, with the Edict of Thessalonica in A.D. 380 came the great change, the identification of the Church with the Imperium. This edict stated in part:

We desire that all peoples who fall beneath the sway of our imperial clemency should profess the Faith which we believe to have been communicated by the apostle Peter. . . . should believe in one deity, the Father, Son, and Holy Spirit . . . should embrace the name of Catholic Christians, adjudging others madmen and heretics . . . to suffer divine punishment and therewith the vengeance of that power which we, by celestial power, have assumed.

After this in the East Byzantine Christianity went on to flourish for many centuries, developing the strange mixture of the Caesaropapism of the State Church and the other-worldly disregard of social conditions which almost two thousand years later contributed to the explosion called the Russian Revolution.

In the West, meanwhile, the structures of pagan Rome were disintegrating. In the confusing changes of that age St. Augustine, classicist and Christian, was developing a new concept of the city, at least a new way of looking at the juxtaposition of the Church and the world. His images became part of the heritage of the West and to this day influence the thinking of the Church, perhaps as much on a subconscious as on a conscious level. St. Augustine portrayed two cities, the "City of God" and the "City of the World." These cities were not to be identified with the

Church and the State but with the saved and the damned. They were indivisibly interwoven, and no one could rightly tell to which each citizen belonged; they interacted, one upon the other. "The two cities [the one of predestinate and the other of reprobate] are in the world confused together and commixed, until the general judgement make a separation." [1]

The City of God was the heavenly Jerusalem ("our citizenship is in heaven"). Although it was not coterminous with the Church, it was symbolized on earth by the Church. It no more took cognizance of the State than a worshiper would notice a policeman on his way to church. While the Augustinian view was not explicitly revolutionary, it did set forth a new institutional loyalty which, by implication, could undermine the authority of the State. Thus in the writings of St. Augustine were sown the seeds of the later great claims of the Popes upon the Emperors, and in the passing of the years the two cities did come to be identified with the Church and the State—not as separate groups of persons, but as separate centers of interest and power.

The present conflict between Church and State in the United States is a continuance of the tensions which St. Augustine defined. Perhaps a clearer understanding of St. Augustine, unblurred by the intervening history which he so deeply influenced, would enable present-day Christians to step outside the too narrow categories of Church and State and solve the problem of religious freedom in a state of godly people.

It is a temptation to dwell on intricacies of the conflict between Church and State, but this is not our objective. There were other institutions in the Middle Ages which still control contemporary thoughts of the Church and the City. Monasticism was an attempt to build a City within society, a City as nearly perfect as man could make it. St. Augustine himself founded a monastic order, but the master builder was St. Benedict. The

[1] St. Augustine, *City of God*, Bk. I, Chap. 34.

perfection of his dream still draws men and women to pursue it, and his rule influences all Western ideas of the good life and, consequently, all Western thinking about that life of men with each other which is called the City. Monasticism was the continuing link between the Middle Ages and the classical world.

So attractive were these manifestations of the Christian life that Joachim of Floris, in the twelfth century, looked forward to a final period of human development, the period of the Holy Ghost, when all mankind would be united, as monastic brethren and sisters, in the Monastery Universal. To Bernard of Clairvaux, in the same century, the cloister was a stronghold of paradise: he even coined the term *paradisus claustralis.*

The closest link between the classic city and the mediaeval city was that formed then, not by the surviving buildings and customs, but by the monastery. . . .

The monasteries kept alive the image of the Heavenly City. As the new urban communities took form after the tenth century, the monastery made an even deeper imprint on their life at first than did the market. Here was the peace and order, the quietness and inwardness beloved by Christian men.[2]

WHEN THE CHURCH WAS THE CITY

Here is a new concept: the thinking of the Church actually shaping the form of the city and its ideals. In that day of universal acknowledgment of the Christian faith it was not a strange concept, but it illuminates the confusion of our present pluralistic society. Our society, having no agreed-upon theology or world view, either ignores the necessity of an undergirding philosophy of the city or struggles hopelessly to make one up out of whole cloth without regard to the metaphysical and religious premises

[2] Lewis Mumford, *The City in History* (New York: Harcourt, Brace, and World, 1961), p. 247.

which must be the foundation of any coherent theory of social life.

The Church shaped not only the institutions of the medieval city's life but, as every European traveler knows, the very physical shape. As each life was under God and each social grouping under his rule, so each town and city dwelt under the shadow of the Cathedral and into the symbolism of that building poured the best of riches and of talent. Within the great stone walls, often as crude and rough as the life around them, were chapels of the artisans, the military, the farmers, and the stonemasons. Each of these institutions took on something of the flavor of the Church of which they felt a part, and the Church was influenced in return. The courage, power, command, and careful delineation of authority found within the cult of the military, for instance, became romanticized into the cult of chivalry which sported the love of Galahad for the Holy Grail in terms not so different from the love of Lancelot for Guinevere.

In the Middle Ages, at least in terms of institutions, the Church *was* the city, sometimes expressed as State, sometimes expressed as Church, but always identified as under God. "With Urabanus (ninth century), one might describe the mediaeval city as a union of Church and community in the pursuit of the Holy Life. Even when it miserably fell short of the Christian ideal, this union nevertheless had produced both institutions and buildings designed to further it." [3]

The separation between Church and State, commerce, or the military was a division of function. Any conflict between them was a conflict of institutions of the same society, not of different societies. Sometimes this conflict was severe. "In the Middle Ages the conflicts between ecclesiastical and especially monastic landlords and the cities were often more severe than those between the cities and secular feudal lords. Outside the Jews, the

[3] *Ibid.*, p. 268.

priesthood was the only alien (outside the law) body within the city after the separation of State and Church in the Investiture struggle." [4]

The medieval city should not be romanticized. The very success of its structure and the resulting wealth which came to the Church undermined the Christian ethic and brought to pass the corruption which made the Reformation inevitable. On the other hand, the identification of the Church with every aspect of city life made the idea of leaving the city, with which we struggle today, impossible. In the medieval city is spelled out the inevitable tension in the work of the Church in the city—the need to be involved in the world without becoming part of the world. The answer can only be found in the mystery of the incarnation. The identity of the Church with her Saviour must be so intense that her involvement with the world does not drag the church away from the redeeming Body of Christ.

The Reformation changed the Church as fundamentally as did Constantine's official recognition of Christianity in an earlier period. At the beginning of the sixteenth century the new power of commerce was being felt around the Cathedral cities and a new division of loyalties was resulting from the emergence of nation states. A new separation of the mind of man accompanied the resurgence of classical knowledge which, although synthesized with Christian doctrine by the Scholastics, could not be completely absorbed and eventually unleashed the forces which formed the pattern of the modern world.

THE CHURCH IN THE CITY

After the Renaissance and the Reformation had run their course, the Church and the city could no longer be identified one with the other. Protestantism was less corrupt than Roman

[4] Max Weber, *The City* (New York: Collier Books, 1962), p. 207.

England became one among many, a gathered Church, to which people came if they chose to worship "decently and in order." The pietism of some Reformation spirituality pushed Christianity back into an individual experience with God. The drive of classical rationalism shattered the already dry theology of the eighteenth century. Certain Reformation movements attempted to reclaim the total city for the Church; notable among them were the theocracy of Calvin's Geneva and the austerity of Hawthorne's Salem. Other Utopian experiments were begun, but these were reminiscent of the monastic withdrawal from the world into a "perfect" community; the Rappites and Owenites of New Harmony, Indiana, were typical of these.

Following hard upon the chaos and vigor of the Reformation came the Industrial Revolution. Whatever success the Church had in dealing with this new phenomenon came largely from the heritage of the Reformation. Despite the disintegrating tendencies (perhaps more effects than causes of the changing society), new strengths came to be present in the Church. Individual responsibility encouraged moral strength; the opening of the Bible to the laity was, and continues to be, an unfailing power for renewal in the life of the Church; and the sense of God's transcendent judgment upon his Church was (and is) a cleansing element. However, such new insights and vigor as the Reformation had brought to the Church were insufficient to enable her to deal with the overwhelming impact of the Industrial Revolution.

Bishop Wickham's study of the Church in Sheffield [5] shows in the microcosm of one city what was happening to the Church in England and, in parallel fashion, slightly delayed, in the United States. He discusses five reasons for the failure of the Church in industrial society.

[5] E. R. Wickham, *Church and People in an Industrial City* (London: Lutterworth Press, 1957), pp. 215ff.

Catholicism at the outset, but because of its diverse
it was less capable of forming society. Instead, by cutt
from the Church of Rome, Protestantism became instit
subservient to the State. *"Cuius regio, cuius religion"*; the
of the king was the religion of the particular nation. In th
following the Renaissance, the so-called Baroque per
State and commerce became the governing forces of
Wren gave the Royal Stock Exchange the position of
his plans for the City of London after the fire; Versaille
archetype of a city planned around the court. No Cathed
had such a vast series of vistas, such gardens stretchin
upon mile, or such fountains and statuary to enshrine it.

As the medieval way of life disintegrated one could b
speak of the work of the Church *in* the city. Even in thos
tries which retained a State Church, the title became a fo
insofar as the actual spiritual life of the community wa
cerned. Although the ideal of the totality of God's inte
the affairs of men, which lay behind the formality, was a
one, history had made its actuality impossible. The Chu
longer *was* the city; the Church, instead, ministered (
glected to minister) *to* the city. We have inherited from
time many of our current problems: Protestant pluralisn
individualism (who is responsible for the unchurched?);
tiplicity of creeds (man chooses his creed, it is not a
thing) leading to secular humanism; institutional encumbr
left over from the days of the identification of the Church
society (what is the role of the parish, what *is* the parish?)
antipathy of the "lower classes" to the traditional churches
cause of their identity with the nobility and later with
bourgeoisie (how can the Church attract the laboring ma

The Church, no longer legally responsible for the whol
society, ceased to feel morally responsible. This irrespons
ity expressed itself in several ways. The State Church

1. *The historic estrangement of the working class.* They had become, with the rise of population, an "undifferentiated group, lost to view except as a mass. This, coupled with the economic rise of a middle class that was increasingly religious in its habit, led to a social stratification in which religious and denominational lines ran parallel to the economic ones, so that the poor were excluded both socially and religiously; a fact that both hardened the separation of classes (even where the edges were blurred) and widened the gulf between the churches and the working classes."

2. *The loss of the middle classes.* "The religious faith of the middle classes had always been weaker than its impressive expression suggested. A faith that is so widely conformist, and in the best sense of the word conventional, and at the same time, whether evangelical or catholic, prone to narrowness and pietism, is ill-equipped to wrestle with a world so heavily secular as the twentieth century was to become. At best it could maintain itself only by isolation from the realities of the time—a possibility not open to the urban middle classes, who were notoriously activist. And in the ensuing dichotomy between religion and the world, the latter was bound to triumph." This has not occurred in the United States to the same extent it has in England, but the analysis of this loss in England may well be prophetic for the United States.

3. *The sociology of faith and unbelief.* Bishop Wickham states his belief that the environment of the industrial worker is inimical to the reception of the gospel. The Church has not attempted to analyze, much less influence, the massive forces, the "principalities and powers," which form this environment.

4. *The lack of prophecy.* Theology has not begun to deal with what is important to the intelligent modern man; it has not come to terms with "the scientific revolution and the social revolution."

5. *The inadequate structure of the Church.* The parochial

structure and the institutional structure of the Church which grew out of medieval society cannot begin to be effective today.

In the Church's ministry to the city there have been particular men and movements who have attempted to meet the difficulties outlined above. They sensed the massive failure of the Church in its ministry to the city as a whole and dared to seek new ways. Not all of these movements were precipitated by the Industrial Revolution. In preceding centuries many had been motivated by a recognition of the Church's failure to minister to the poor and dispossessed and, although they were not "city men," their ideas clearly influenced later urban ministries.

St. Francis of Assisi, in the thirteenth century, was a child of the high mercantilism of his age. In the midst of the color and glory of his rich and cavalier life came the Christ-vision, radical and demanding. The locus of the vision was the poor and dispossessed, its sacramental embodiment the face of the leper. St. Francis courted Lady Poverty in a holy burlesque of courtly love; he fought through the glory of charity with the courage of chivalry to the very end, where he found the agonized but joyful victory of the stigmata.

St. Benedict had previously established at Monte Cassino, not far from Assisi, a city within a city as a means of reaching beyond the ministry of the conventional life of the Church, but St. Francis infiltrated the city with a nomadic community whose only bond was the love of Jesus. He typifies the evangelical spirit, impatient with the encumbrances of the institutional church, which periodically breaks out in search of a new way to bring Christ to those to whom he had long been hidden by the very Church which had purported to be his Body.

Others followed the example of St. Francis, each teaching in a different spirit, but each seeking a new way of involvement. Dominic, Ignatius of Loyola, and John Wyclif closely identified with the social issues of their day. These and many others sought and found new ways. They were not "city men" per se, but their ideas influenced later urban movements and they included the city, quite naturally, within their area of concern.

BEGINNINGS OF URBAN EVANGELISM

It is amazing how quickly the Church of England settled into a calm institutional life after the turmoil of the Reformation and civil war. This relative quiet flowed thin and undisturbed until an evangelical zeal broke into the strange and troubled spirit of John Wesley. The church from which he sprang was not only socially unconcerned and so conventional that the poor could not feel comfortable within it; it was also spiritually unalive, aristocratic in make-up, and very close to deism in theology. Wesley preached a personal and emotional relationship with Jesus the Saviour. He made no attempt to be an instrument of direct social action; in fact, he worked clearly within the class structure of England. Yet his thirst for souls encompassed all souls and the new structure of the open-air meetings and Bible classes cut across class lines. Such is the force of habit, however, that Methodism soon lost its genius for new forms, became more and more an institutional church, and finally excluded the poor even more effectively than the Church of England. In many parts of America, especially in the Midwest, where it is strong, Methodism resembles the Church of England as a social institution of conservatism within the community to a greater extent than does the Episcopal Church.

Looking back on Wesley in England and the courageous Circuit Riders of America, one may well ask why there are no more of their kind. What happened to the pioneering spirit of Methodism? Was it drained off in foreign missions, leaving only the less adventurous and inventive at home? Is there any way to cultivate and encourage the springing up of religious genius, of radical movements within the Church? Must we wait upon the Spirit to do the improbable—to visit a medieval soldier imprisoned in an Italian town, or to find a confused Church of England missionary in the midst of a storm-tossed Atlantic hearing the Word as sung by his Moravian fellow travelers?

In the nineteenth century there was something of a religious revival (with a small "r") in England and America. In the high Victorian Age church-going became popular. It was conventional and formal, a status symbol unequaled in modern times, except perhaps in the suburban America of today. This church attendance was a middle-class phenomenon for the most part. It did not reach the "poor," who seemed to be cut off from the Church by the factors of the sociology of the Industrial Age, if one accepts Bishop Wickham's analysis.

Beneath the moralism of Victorian Christianity were present some significant movements of the Spirit. The great reform movements of antislavery both in England and in the United States were inspired by Christians. A social consciousness promoted the organization of chapels for the poor in England and America, the settlement movement, and the founding of great institutional parishes like St. George's in New York. The Social Gospel of Walter Rauschenbusch attested to the realization on the part of the Victorians that the gospel could not be denied to the poor and that conditions which made men less than the children of God could not be ignored.

Whatever the theology and churchmanship within which a valid movement of the Spirit clothes itself, it will seek out the souls of men within the dispossessed and the socially oppressed. The Oxford Movement in America has been known until recently as a liturgical and devotional movement, with a few exceptionally great figures like Father Huntington in his early days. But in England its followers first won the deep, if grudging, respect of the Church at large through their intellectual ability and, even more important, through their valiant ministry in the slums of London. Wesley formed new structures; the priests of the Oxford Movement brought a theology new to the Church of England into the parish structure. They "aped" Rome, to be sure, and practiced liturgical habits at which the liturgical movement enthusiasts of today turn up their noses; yet their zeal and their love for Jesus shone through the most slavish of these imitations.

Charles Lowder first earned the title "Father" for the Anglican clergy as his people watched his fearless ministry during a plague in the London dock area. At St. Peter's, London Docks, a window shows him carrying a stricken child in his arms. Father Wainwright, vicar of the same parish, never spent a night outside his parish bounds. Father Jellicoe, long before the era of McCarthyism, was branded a Communist because of his fierce battle for better housing in East London. These were men of the city, incarnational, sacramental Catholics, living out the gospel with the Christ of the altar and the Christ of the poor. They have had followers and have inspired later efforts; yet too often their parishes under less inspired devotion have lapsed back into shrines of "high church" devotees or meeting places for a few frightened people.

In this rather arbitrary selection of historical material, some of the generalizations may be subject to criticism. But perhaps enough has been said to make us aware of the heritage of power the Church has at her command through the examples of history —and of the vast freightage of encumbrances which may have to be ruthlessly chopped away if the Church is to become once more a significant force in the life of the city.

3. The Church and the Modern City

IN AMERICA, at the turn of this century the so-called "social gospel" led many wealthy churches to establish chapels in the slums—enterprises full of good works but chary of mixing the old congregation and the new. This too-safe paternalism, however, wore itself out to a large extent, so that in the twenties and thirties countless churches of all denominations in run-down neighborhoods were sold, and in the metropolitan areas the non-Roman churches became identified with suburbia, Park Avenue, and the big downtown parish.

The reasons for this retreat from the depressed areas of the cities were twofold: migration of church members to the suburbs and the lack of an urban mission philosophy. When the church members who once lived in these urban neighborhoods migrated, a variety of other peoples moved in: Roman Catholics—Irish, German, Polish—poured into the metropolitan areas of the East, followed in turn by Southern Negroes of Baptist, Methodist, and Pentecostal background, and, more recently, by Puerto Ricans with a Roman Catholic cultural heritage. In the Southwest, Roman Catholic Mexicans came in; to the Middle West moved Baptist and Pentecostal up-country farmers of Kentucky and Tennessee; in the Far West were the Orientals.

The churches followed their members to their new residential areas—or, more accurately, the new suburbanites brought their churches with them. The emptying downtown church buildings remained. Huge structures, like the Church of the Advocate in Philadelphia, towered above thickly settled areas of Negro people but ministered to a handful of commuting whites. Smaller churches, like St. Mark's, Jersey City, closed down. It was clear that the churches of both Anglican and Reform traditions were retreating from the inner city as the people of non-English heritage moved in.

There were classical exceptions to this trend. St. Philip's and St. Martin's parishes in Harlem continued strong. Their people had not moved out in any considerable numbers, and they continued to be augmented by new arrivals with an Anglican West Indian background. The large downtown church like Trinity Church in New York frequently remained in rather good shape. Its classic location in the center of town, its accessibility to bus lines and large hotels, its ability to supplement its Sunday mission with a weekday ministry, and its large endowment and historical role better enabled it to survive the inroads of moving population. A few institutional churches like Christ Church, Cincinnati, continued strong while also conducting an effective neighborhood ministry. But in general the Church was in retreat from the city.

When we look back now, it is not too hard to see what a tragic mistake this flight from the city was. Indeed, only fairly recently has the full import of that mismove revealed itself. No one has brought it to the attention of the Church more forcefully than did Truman Douglas when he declared: "In almost direct proportion to the increasing importance of the city in American culture has been the withdrawal—both physical and spiritual— of the Protestant Church. If Protestantism gives up the city, it virtually gives up America. Yet that is precisely what it has been doing."

The awakening of the churches to the situation began after

World War II but has proceeded rather slowly. A major difficulty, of course, has been that the churches lacked an urban mission theology and the techniques with which to implement it. Inner-city work has had to be experimental and slow because of the nature of the problem. Today a number of churches can report fairly successful projects, but urban work still has a long way to go. No attempt will be made here to present the total picture, but the story of the development of an inner-city program and theology in the Episcopal Church will illustrate perhaps some dimensions of the new approach. In other chapters we shall examine specifically some individual projects churches have undertaken.

After World War II, various groups in the Episcopal Church spontaneously began to look for a positive approach to the inner-city situation. In Pittsburgh, under the leadership of Bishop Pardue, the Society for the Promotion of Industrial Missions was attacking with vigor the gradual demise of our church in the mill and mining towns near Pittsburgh. They attempted to relate the Church to a man's work and to his life as a trade-union member. The Urban Priests' Group began to meet informally in the New York area. Their chief concern was a missionary outreach to the so-called slum areas of metropolitan New York and New Jersey. A quasi-official conference on the urban church was held in Chicago about 1950 under the auspices of the Episcopal Urban Fellowship. In 1950 the House of Bishops set up a division of Urban-Industrial Work, under National Council's Department of Christian Social Relations, the sole responsibility of which would be to encourage urban study and coordinate the Church's ministry to the city. These were some of the straws in the wind as the 1950's ushered in a new concern for the Church in the city. We had finally come to realize that the city was the greatest missionary challenge our church had ever faced, and that the very innermost life of the Church had to be examined to understand why our church had ceased to speak to so many.

Picture yourself as the rector of a small city church. You graduated from a good seminary. People have told you that your sermons are effective. You follow the suggestions for parish management coming from the National Council. Yet, month by month, your congregation dwindles. What is wrong?

Or picture yourself as the rector of a thriving suburban parish, throbbing with coffee hours and scout troops. Yet whenever you suggest a prayer group or intensive Bible study, whenever you attempt to lead the congregation into an awareness of responsibility toward social problems on their doorstep, the response is sickening. Somehow, somewhere along the line our church had ceased to communicate with the people. In the inner city the people just plain did not come. In the suburbs they came, but they certainly were not, for the most part, caught up in the City of God. Two sides of the same coin!

Various groups have been searching for answers in church history and in the thought of the Church abroad; have been working, thinking, talking, and praying about the daily problems of the parish ministry in exurbia, mill town, or slum. They have not established clear-cut doctrinal positions. Their thought overlaps in many of its phases. They have published very little. And yet it is most important for the Church as a whole to be aware of these springs of new life. Thus, in the following pages, we shall attempt to outline the thinking which focuses around some of these groups, realizing the treatment to be inadequate but hoping that it will stimulate more churchmen seriously to consider our task—to redeem the city of man, to establish the City of God.

THE URBAN PRIESTS

Postwar France has been a scene of religious revitalization within the Roman Catholic Church. Young priests and laymen had endured the catastrophe of the war and had found depths of meaning in the underground and in prison camps. Henri Perrin, a priest, found the atoning power of Christ's suffering when he celebrated Mass secretly in the latrine of a German concentration camp. Members of the lay Jocist movement, having lived close to death for reasons of freedom and patriotism, now sought a similar intensity in their religious life and witness. But in the institutional Church of France apathetic, bourgeois attitudes prevailed. The story is told of a small community of newly converted Roman Catholics, disciples of a priest who expressed his vocation as a factory worker, who for the first time attended Mass at a parish church. They sat through the chaos, coldness, and impersonality of the scene as the celebrant mumbled in Latin and a few elderly folk rattled their beads; they waited patiently, and finally, guilelessly asked their priest, "Where are the Christians?"

It was against the softness and irrelevance within the church that these new Christians addressed themselves. Or rather, they sought to win the proletariat to Christ despite the church. The gap in the mores between factory worker and parish life was too great; the members of the new movement sought to change the life of the parish so that it made sense to the worker[1] or to reach that worker through extraparochial methods by *identifying* themselves with him[2]—sharing his life, thoughts, feelings, work, trade-union, and even his political views. In order to strengthen

[1] George Michonneau, *Revolution in a City Parish* (Westminster, Md.: Newman Press, 1950).

[2] Jacques Loew, *Mission to the Poorest* (New York: Sheed & Ward, 1950).

such an attempt, to keep it from foundering, those involved felt the need of an intense community life. They found, too, as Christians through the ages have found, that a vital Christian community was necessary to any full-scale evangelism. The convert must be brought *into* something which is alive and different and exciting. He must be able to experience Christianity in the love of a human community for him as a person and thereby come to know the love of Christ in his Body, the Church.

These, to a student of the missionary history of Christianity, are clearly not new ideas, but they spoke forcibly to the lonely and broken twentieth-century man. And it was with the inspiration of the experiences of the Church in France, as well as a fresh reading of the accounts of the dockside parishes of London earlier in the century, that the clergy who later comprised the Urban Priests began their ministry in the depressed areas of New York and Jersey City.

America is not France. There is not so clear a cleavage between proletariat and bourgeoisie. However, there is an analogy to this situation. *The Episcopal Church in its present cultural form is set up to minister primarily to the white Protestant middle-class American*—those of at least high-school education and of either Anglo-Saxon or third-generation American background. To this group is communication geared on the levels of language, ideas, and emotions. This is true of tracts, organizations, Christian education materials, liturgical practices, and hymnody. Therefore, to some extent, the Episcopal Church is faced with the same problem of communication as the Roman Catholic Church of France, when she ministers to the less educated groups of the depressed areas of the inner city; formal, Anglican religion faces Southern Negroes, Puerto Ricans, Mexicans, Orientals, Kentucky farmers, Italians, Irish, and the other culturally different dwellers of the tenements. None of these people is caught up by, or can feel sympathetic to, the restrained orderliness of classical Anglicanism which is so much a product of English culture. How then can we divest cultural appendages from the Church so that she can reach people of a different ethos? Or, rephrasing the question: can the cumbersome, dignified, proper, and occasionally overrespectable Episcopal Church reach the throbbing life of a city slum?

The Urban Priests' answer to this is Yes! If we are the Holy Catholic Church we can and will reach all people, even if it means working out with the guidance of the Holy Spirit a very different kind of parish life.

The beginning of a renewed full-scale effort to reach the inner city was made at Grace Church (van Vorst), Jersey City, in 1949. The Lower East Side of New York, Boston, Philadelphia, Dallas, and South Florida soon were scenes of similar efforts. In 1953 the Urban Mission Priests drew up a *Statement of Aims and Principles* in which they stated their objectives of promoting and bringing into the Church the residents of the inner city, as well as "raising up" leadership which would be concerned with the great social issues of the day.

What was the new philosophy behind this missionary outreach?

CHRISTIAN COMMUNITY

The Urban Priests' group felt that the foundation of urban work must be Christian community, expressed in a life shared by the clergy and laity of the staff. They felt that even such a small group, living together as Christians, could soon find guidance from the Holy Spirit; and that out of the intimate eating, praying, and working together of such a team *does* come guidance. How could people be taught to love each other if there were no example to follow? How else could there be strength to sustain the overwhelming discouragement of a large, empty church, of poverty and suffering on the part of parishioners, of the continual wear and tear of slum life as it came from every quarter?

The Christian community is an open community offering its warmth to any who wish to come in. A ragged little boy peeks in the window day after day. He finally comes in and timidly accepts a sandwich. He asks, with wonder in his eyes, "Does this mean I really belong?" Another, running away from an intolerable situation, comes as far as the rectory and moves in for a while. A family with ten children is burned out, and four of the boys stay in the rectory. A girl, pregnant and unmarried, with nowhere to go, unself-consciously passes many afternoons in the living room or helps with the dishes. These are things which happen occasionally in every rectory, but in the inner-city parish they happen continually, overwhelmingly, if the door is open and there is warmth inside. The warmth can only continue warm, the load of sharing can only be sustained, if Christ can exist within a group, a community, to carry it. It is cold and lonely outside; a living community of joy and love attracts people. And once they are drawn in, it is but a short step from the kitchen table to the altar, from the jokes and concern of the household to the hymns and liturgy of the Church.

THE LITURGY

A great deal of the thinking of the Urban Priests' group stems from the liturgical movement, a school of thought which endeavors to reawaken the Church to the power of the liturgy.[3] Worship, and especially the Eucharist, is the heart of the life of the community. Unless Christ lives within the community the friendships become conflicts, the love becomes irritation and even hate. And Christ lives supremely by promise in the community through his Eucharistic Presence, as the Christians gather

[3] The Associated Parishes, Inc., 6 North Carroll Street, Madison 3, Wisconsin, have been instrumental in doing this in the Episcopal Church.

again and again to absorb the pattern and the power of his Kingdom. See how this works.

It is a Wednesday evening in the middle of Lent. The parish gathers at 8:oo PM for the midweek family Eucharist. In off the street they come—large and small, dark and white, Spanish, Chinese, Italian, children and their families dressed in Sunday clothes, children alone in dirty clothes. A Bowery character, ill-clad, comes in for a few minutes to warm himself and snooze in the back pew. The church is a contrast to the city around it and preserves a stately Victorian beauty; at the door a priest welcomes the stranger, and the dignity of the architecture warms to the presence of the people. The service opens with a familiar hymn while the procession enters and the priests follow a motley crew of acolytes.

They take their places behind the altar, facing the congregation, clad in bold, contemporary liturgical vestments cut and sewn by a member of the parish. The words of the prayers may partly escape the people, but there are actions; there is a sweeping rhythm to the liturgy, explained by a priest as it progresses. The gospel procession forms and proceeds down to the center of the congregation as it must go forth to the center of the world; the offertory procession comes up from the back, bearing the lives of the people in the alms, the bread and wine, their work and play, and their sorrow and joy. The communicants come to know that their offering, given in penitence and sincerity, is as important to God as the greatest contribution the Church can receive and that they offer it as a community only when the lifeblood of each is, as it were, mixed with the lifeblood of his neighbor as a symbol of Christian love at its deepest and most radical. Only then, when all are joined in love, can Christ say, "This is *my Body;* this is *my Blood.*" It is on this level that a theology of relations between people is worked out. There can be no separation; the blood of our brothers runs through our veins. A Christian fellowship continually reminded of this cannot long sustain barriers between black and white, rich and poor. As the fusion occurs a great energy is set loose, and an unexpected dynamism enlivens the community life.

The Prayer for the Church includes the world and is added to this offering. And finally, in the Prayer of Consecration all is made holy; the squalor, the poverty, the humility, the insults, and the condescension: all this is offered now in the great sacrifice of the Cross; disgrace and death become glory and resurrection. Words may not be understood, but who can mistake the meaning of the final elevation of the Host—the climax of all, the sanctifying and ennobling of life offered in glory with the "one, true, pure, immortal sacrifice"?

The Communion is received; the communicants next to each other with hands extended, blessed children receiving their food from God. There is no deeper psychological action than receiving love as food, no closer parallel in worship to the new insights that mind and body and soul are one, or no clearer healing power of psyche than this great acceptance of each soul into the heart of the universe.

The Eucharist is the acting out of the perfect community in love of God. To the altar is brought the created world, the broken lives, and the broken society; from the altar the people go forth to bring this loving action into the world. And it is in the liturgy and the sacramental view of life that the doctrine and dynamic, the pattern and the power, for social action is shown forth. The sacramental view seeks to sanctify and redeem the space-time world, finding in all material things a visible sign of the Word of God. It is a showing forth of the already indwelling Christ in daily life; and in the showing forth there comes to pass a deepening of this indwelling. In the Sacrament the pastoral ministry begins, and in the Sacrament those who are to labor for this showing forth in social action find strength.

THE PASTORAL MINISTRY

The cure of souls is concerned with the *total person.* In attempting to meet the overwhelming pastoral problems of the depressed areas, penance, unction, and the Holy Communion may be used along with the "therapy" of life in an accepting community and the "acceptance" and sharing of burdens. Referral in as professional a way as possible to other social agencies, the use of skilled social workers when available, and the attempt, through social action, to remove the cause of illness: all these healing resources are also brought to bear in a spirit of love to heal the whole person in his total environment of family, housing, neighborhood, work, and Church.

SOCIAL ACTION

The community finds its dynamic within the liturgy and within its daily life together; and from its own needs the community is guided to a course not only of pastoral work, but of social action. Let us take an example. A family in the Sunday School is to be evicted for nonpayment of illegally raised rent. The Church gives them advice as to their rights with the landlord and the morale to fight him. The housing problem, however, is also seen to lie far beyond an individual house. The community becomes involved in eliminating discrimination in public housing. Thus the work of social action proceeds from the *needs* of members of the community, through the *action* of members of the community, until its leavening process affects the city surrounding the church in ever widening circles. Or, one of the children is beaten by the police. Such an incident involved Grace Church in Jersey City in a long struggle for better police methods, public recreation, and all the steps needed to lessen juvenile delinquency. Carrying out such programs takes perseverance and frequently real courage to withstand threats by politicians against one's job or home.

St. Augustine's in New York has become deeply involved in the gang problem of the Lower East Side. St. Mark's in Chicago has pioneered in setting up a narcotics clinic. St. Augustine's, Dallas, sought to heal the segregation of three racially separated housing projects within which it was located. St. John's, Roxbury, Massachusetts, and its neighboring parishes have arranged a corporate effort to meet community problems. The urban parishes in Indianapolis are investigating the needs of the people in downtown neighborhoods. And through it all is the theme of bringing the surrounding neighborhood in all its phases a little closer to the Kingdom of God as revealed in the action of the Eucharist.

CONCLUSION

There are other characteristics of many of the parishes connected with the Urban Priests' group—joy, humor, foolishness, or a combination of these. The rectories involved are usually full of laughter. No one is ever surprised at the things that happen— the street processions, the play with children on the street, the cleaning up of back yards by priests in clerical collars, jitterbug contests in the living room, finding someone asleep in the confessional, circulating petitions in housing projects, or making speeches on street corners—all these things combine being "a fool for Christ's sake" and merely "having a wonderful time" being Christians. And so the pathos is tempered with joy in an approximation of the Franciscan spirit.

This spirit is not only in the parish itself, but one finds it in many of the people living under conditions of poverty. And one of the most important of the ideals of the urban parish is for the clergy to identify as much as possible with the people whom they serve. They must, when physically possible, live in the neighborhood, share the neighborhood's problems, and even, in taking them on, be willing to be torn apart by the neighborhood conflicts.

People must come to understand that a parish not in tension is not, in our day, a Christian parish. . . . More than not, the [tension or] crisis is present but unrecognized. Whenever there is a rift in the human relations between persons or groups in a parish there is a crisis—the Advent of God in the Holy Eucharist is "breaking through" although in a sometimes hidden way. Whenever there are people in a town designated as those "on the other side of the tracks," there is a crisis present. Whenever a brown-skinned person is given the cold shoulder in a parish church, the time of crisis has arrived. The web of love relationships has been broken and it is time for confession. . . . the Church must take the World into its arms while still continuing to fight it.[4]

It may be that since the City is the symbol of redeemed humanity and the heavenly Jerusalem, the unredeemed city is more demonic than any other social grouping, because it is perverted good. And it seems that the closer people live to one another, the more intense are the results of the sin that separates. Thus, the social problems of Spanish Harlem are worse than the same kind of problems in Jersey City, because the latter is less densely populated. A city is, after all, a series of interlocking relationships, husband to wife, lover to beloved, parent to child, boss to employee, landlord to tenant, and priest to parishioner. It is the purpose of the urban parish to redeem these relationships, praying for them at the altar, sending forth healing strength into them from the altar of God, even "the God of my joy and gladness."

From the philosophy and purpose of the Urban Mission Priests has evolved an active program. Some concrete evidence of the results are seen in the individual social actions of members, summer training programs for college and seminary students, "Seminary Associate" promotions in some seminaries to stimulate vocations in this area, and an Urban Laymen's Group.

[4] C. Kilmer Myers, *Light the Dark Streets* (New York: Seabury Press, 1958), pp. 150-152.

This latter group has essentially the same philosophy as the Urban Mission Priests, and its members propose to assist their parish priests in discovering ways and means of implementing these basic concepts. While looking to the clergy for spiritual leadership and guidance, they recognize that "the ultimate goal is full participation by the laity on all levels of activity." (See Appendix A.)

This is an example of the kind of concern on the part of the laity which is evident throughout the Church. One of the most interesting developments in regard to this "priesthood of the laity" is in evidence at Parishfield, where the dynamics of Christian community are being explored. Under the leadership of the Reverend Francis Ayres several clergy and their families have lived and worshiped together in what has become a conference center outside Detroit. They have sought to reconsider the concepts of the parish and of the ministry of the laity. Through the guidance of the Spirit there has developed a new sense of the problems the Church faces today as she attempts to redeem the fast-changing society around her.

DETROIT INDUSTRIAL MISSION

One of the outgrowths of this thinking is now a separate entity known as the Detroit Industrial Mission (DIM), which seeks an answer to the same general problem we have been discussing, namely, that the Church is not reaching the modern American in his total life. As the Urban Priests have sought to adapt the Church to the conditions of the inner city, the DIM seeks to adapt the Church as a whole to the industrial society of today. The aim is to bring Christianity out of the churches into the world of men at their work. To quote from its Statement of Purpose:

A "new society" of large-scale industrial organization has grown up in America in the last half-century that was as unknown to the Founding Fathers as the jet airplane and the atomic bomb. . . . The Detroit Industrial Mission through research, study, experimentation, and training is attempting to evolve a better understanding of man's problems in his work situation. . . . Since most of life is spent in earning a living, we believe that workers in all categories need to realize the relationship between Christianity and their own work.

Among the appealing qualities of the DIM are its realism and humility. One of the staff, who spent some time working in similar work in Sheffield, England, states the spirit of DIM as it approaches industrial management: "We have some knowledge of the Bible and a bit of theological understanding. You, however, know far more about industry and its problems than we do. Maybe we can pool our knowledge and carry on such a fruitful discussion that together we can see how Christianity can both enrich the life of industry and contribute significantly to the solution of its problems."

The DIM is a good example of imaginative leadership by a bishop. These new ventures must have strong episcopal backing to be effective. This, in turn, means backing by the church at large.

THE CHURCH IN URBAN INDUSTRY

Perhaps the most important rallying point for the new thinking of the Church in this field was the Urban Industrial Division of National Council's Department of Christian Social Relations. Under imaginative leadership and with the backing of an informed board of clergy and laymen, the division constantly upheld the ideal of radical and courageous rethinking of the Church's position in the city. Twenty research projects were set up whereby a particular aspect of the Church's ministry to the city was experimented upon and reported.

Many interesting and unexpected insights were gained, many "reproducible techniques" passed along. St. John's, Roxbury, Massachusetts had a storefront center; Reno, a specialized clinic in counseling divorcees; Seattle, a project in child evangelism; Schenectady, a study of parish involvement in a *rapprochement* between management and labor. The division sponsored numerous conferences and had a special project in bringing the skills of the seminaries into a fruitful relationship with these new insights. The most valuable insight of all is that whenever a "tough" problem is recognized as a missionary challenge rather than a symptom of failure, the morale of the parish changes, and even though the problem may not be solved, the parish comes to life.

A particular interest of the Urban Industrial Division was the study of motivation. Using the new knowledge provided by motivational research, publicized recently in such books as Vance Packard's *Hidden Persuaders*, the church seeks to find on the deepest psychological level *why* people come to church and *why* they stay away. The danger of this approach, of course, is using a person's psychological needs rather than the Word of God as the guiding principle in the Church's program. But, if this danger is acknowledged, we can reach new levels of effective appeal and communication through this area of study.[5]

The General Convention of 1961 in Detroit dramatized the urban civilization in which we are living. The setting was Cobo Hall in the center of Detroit's waterfront redevelopment. The scale of the building, the plate glass windows through which ships of every nation could be seen sailing up the river to the Great Lakes, and the old Mariner's church which had survived the radical change in the scene made even the most conservative of delegates aware of the changes overtaking the Church and

[5] Much of the experience of the division is described in *The Church on the Urban Frontier*, by G. Paul Musselman (New York: Seabury Press, 1960).

society. Two developments in the business of the convention are worthy of note.

The Detroit Industrial Mission, in cooperation with The Joint Commission on the Ministry to Industrial Areas, sponsored a tour of convention delegates to the assembly line of Detroit and then showed a movie projecting the problems of the industrial worker trying to find significance in the life of the Church. The Church and City Conference, a fellowship of clergy from old downtown churches, sponsored a dinner; their principal interest was the work of the Church in the city, and at several informal gatherings they outlined the program which they hoped would be accepted by the convention for the ensuing triennial. The response was enthusiastic and heartening.

Out of the convention came a program for the national Church and the allocation of over $300,000 for urban work. The program would now be administered through the Home Department, with cooperative work in the Department of Christian Social Relations, the former educational and catalytic, the latter centered on research and concentration on the problems of the individual in urban society. As this book is being written, these plans are only beginning to take shape, but it would seem that there will be concentration on a series of conferences throughout the Church leading to the establishment of diocesan urban committees; other conferences on specialized and sectional problems; consultative services for dioceses and parishes with urban problems; and the promulgating of material taken from work already done throughout the Episcopal Church and other churches.

It is hoped that after this initial program, the Home Department will have a permanent staff of field workers who will be on call for consultation. Perhaps the biggest problem will be the staffing of the department and the conferences with experienced men.

4. Notes on a Theology of Urban Work

"Almighty and most merciful God, who by the glorious Incarnation and Atonement of Christ Jesus hast made men capable of eternal life: Increase among us the knowledge of the exchanges of Thy love, and from the common agony of our lives redeem us to the universal joy of Thy only City: through the . . . mediation of the same Jesus Christ our Lord and Savior, Amen."

—CHARLES WILLIAMS

DID St. Francis consult some medieval sociologist to determine whether he would find transients on the roadside between Assisi and Siena? Did St. Benedict develop the monastery and its rule from the findings of group psychologists? Did our Lord, for that matter, determine the Way of the Cross as the only answer to the power structure of Jerusalem? It was out of the identity of Jesus and Jahweh that the Kingdom was founded in the destruction of Jerusalem; it was out of the simplicity of purpose in St. Benedict's soul that the new vocation of work and prayer was developed; it was the face of Christ in the leper that called St. Francis. The failure of the Church in the city has been a failure, not of technique, but of theology.

Perhaps a new St. Francis or St. Benedict is needed, but it is up to us to understand, as they did, the nature of the Church and its work so that we too may be open to the workings of the Spirit. Important as techniques may be (no one was more aware of the importance of detail than St. Benedict), they are worthless if the purpose for which they are used is not God's purpose for his Church.

It is difficult to pinpoint the source of the failure of nerve and of heart which has been witnessed in the great cities of America. In attempting to do so, it is all too easy to disparage the heroism of the lonely priest with his handful of laymen manning the last rampart with broken weapons. The failure of the heart is not his; it is in the whole body of the Church which allows him to struggle on unassisted and ill-advised. Our contention is that this failure results from neglecting the traditional doctrine of the Holy Catholic Church; that neglect has cut her off from her essential nourishment and has sapped her vitality.

Various heresies have played their part in this failure at various times in history—the Pelagianism of the late Middle Ages, the individualism springing from the Protestant Reformation, the near-deism of the eighteenth-century Anglican Church, the puritanism of American Christianity. Each of these has been a strand to bind the Church, and each continues to fetter her today. Merely blasting away at heresy is an easy pursuit, but it is also a relatively useless one. Instead, let us look briefly once more at the great truths of the faith held up before the modern city.

The usual approach to a theology of urban work has been a pragmatic one, an attempt to discover the seeming needs of the people of the city and then to apply the appropriate theological poultice. Norman Vincent Peale with his peace cult tries to meet the anxiety of the day; the Urban Mission Priests of New York strive to meet the desperation of slum housing with their theology of social action. The needs of urban man are important; but no matter how valid they may be, man's needs cannot *de-*

termine theological principle. To assume so is a basic fallacy, a misunderstanding encouraged by the existential climate of the day.

Our approach in this chapter will be to touch upon the great dogmas of the Church and to indicate their application. This, hopefully, will give a total and balanced framework within which, in the dialogue of God's action and man's response, we will find an ever-deepening understanding of our mission. We seek an existential experience of knowledge in which God will be known as more than a mere tool.

CREATION

The creation myth still dwells in the depths of man. The beauty of a rural summer evening, the kinship of a man and his dog, the Freudian symbolism of the apple and the serpent, the resurgence in every age of a noble savage philosophy of one kind or another: such things attest to our deep involvement with Eden. This romanticism is rife in the Church, although it appears in hidden form. The pipe-smoking parson is beloved as an echo of rural England, as is the archetypal vicar fishing the trout stream after tea. Old churches (even imitation old churches) help turn the dynamism of the psyche backward to a comfortable regression in archaeology and antiquarianism, to the beauty of ruins and the safety of the past. There is something rather comfortable in Adam and his most understandable sin. Whatever the reasons, the eyes of the Church are cast backward. The thinking of the Church about creation too often concerns itself with what God *did* in the beauty of Eden or with what men *did* long ago in the golden age of medieval England.

Let the dead bury the dead! Creation is now! It is *now* that God holds in sway the universe, the light years, and the stars. It is now that his eternal creativity spawns ever-new variety of form. Now we, made in his image, channel upon his inanimate creation whatever part of his form is not twisted out of all recognition. The vision of the Kingdom is a City toward which the power of creation thrusts *forward*.

Man is made in the image of God, and no small part of that image is his creativity. Is there any reason to take for granted that the surge of power man now demonstrates does not have as its base this same image? It seems that we always find ourselves fighting the modern city, bemoaning its existence. Those who are building the cities of our day sense this negativism. We who wish to speak to them have no theology of city planning and no sacramental vision of the City. Perhaps a re-examination of the doctrine of creation and man's co-creativity with God should go beyond the neo-Ghandian desire to return to the handcraft of the preindustrial ages, beyond do-it-yourself therapy. It should go beyond insistence on good housing and proper working conditions to an urbanism founded upon the principles of God's creation, or at least to an urbanism redeemed into the shape of his Kingdom. This vision and purpose could give zest and life to the Church's role in the ongoing creation of the city. Then we could share emotionally the enthusiasms of the builders and find with them, perhaps, other than short-term economic goals.

In every city there is a group of men who are shaping the future of that city. Often they are unconscious of their role; always they are being shaped by impersonal economic and sociological forces beyond their control. Nevertheless, they make decisions in a forum of ideas: in the board rooms of industry, in the city council, in the ongoing tension between the idealism of the city planner and the pragmatism of the Chamber of Commerce. Here is a lay ministry: to discover the theological principles involved and to apply to the shape of things to come such principles as diversity in unity (the Trinity) and personhood within community (the Communion of Saints). Such a ministry can be backed by the power of a Church which has its representatives in every related institution and which has come to realize that the modern metropolis need not be a Babylon. Let the Church, then, sense her role in the creation of the city in which she dwells!

INCARNATION

The two great movements of God to the world are those of creation and redemption: the one originating and continuing to empower, the other penetrating and returning the broken and twisted bits to the order and love of God. Let us look at the gentle method of redemption. God first stands afar off, transcendent to his people, ruling from a distance, as it were—Lawgiver, Father, History-maker of the Old Covenant.

The next step of his penetration of the world, the incarnation, is taken only after centuries of preparation. This, in all its implications, comes to be understood only gradually, as if men could not dare to realize it fully. First Jesus seems a wise rabbi, then the Son of God incarnate in a human being; finally the frightening mystery of his taking on humanity as a whole is seen. Christians find themselves members of his Church and thereby members of his Body. The penetration continues to be realized even further as the whole weight of the Eucharist falls upon the Church. It was easy enough to be children of a Father, possible even to endure from time to time the membership in his Body, the Church. But how can one endure and come to terms with the intimate action of the Eucharist, the consuming of the holy flesh, the burning resurrected flesh taken in the mouth? How can one begin to deal with the forced intimacy of the Offertory, in which the lives and the blood of the offerers are churned together?

He came down from heaven, arching into the lives of men. He came down from heaven as a child, a man, a sacrifice. He comes down from heaven now to appear as the Bread of Life and also, sacramentally, in the face, voice, and body of every human being. His movement is down and out: Grace descending, Grace pouring forth. (The Church so often has blocked or gone against this holy stream with a movement inward and upward: "Bring them into the Church, and send them up to heaven.") Redemption is a circular rhythm of return to God; if the Church blocks the outflow of Grace she cannot be the channel of return.

The city is a place of human contact, contact with hundreds of thousands of men, women, and children. They rub shoulders, exchange goods, shout in snarled traffic, and bend in the rhythm of the dance. They engage in conversation, measure justice one upon the other, or merely see numerous others in masses beyond comprehension. The limited creature withdraws in fear from the impossibility of love to all these; the fallen creature twists the relationship. Justice becomes oppression, exchange becomes expropriation, love becomes lust, and conversation becomes monologue. Only the incarnate love of Almighty God can begin to mend these broken loves, to redeem these bent relationships. This incarnate love needs to be incarnate still in the hands and feet, the eyes and mouths of his people. It operates not only through words or the mere manipulation of institutions, but through the loving touch of person to person—touch of feeling, touch of flesh, incarnate touch—through an outgoing Church.

Thus it is that the two most important words in urban work are *involvement* and *identification*. Let us look at the word involvement. Everyone has seen the lonely citadels of worship, their past elegance towering above the past glory of their neighborhoods, with their locked iron gates and their inviolable walls of withdrawal, through which only a handful of old, clean Anglo-Saxons dare to pass. Now one sees more and more these citadels of cleanliness placed in a spot of more elaborate fortification, the antiseptic suburb. There blocks of ranch-type dwellings provide a more effective barrier than the highest iron fence.

These churches, whether in city or suburb, have indeed withdrawn. They have denied their involvement with the pulsing life of the city. Downtown the Church has very few people; in the suburbs there are many people, but the Church is involved with very little of their lives. In both is a denial of the movement of the incarnation. The Church must imitate her Incarnate Lord, must act out her "Bodiness" by becoming involved with every aspect of the life of every human being. The important thing is that, once involved, the Spirit will guide her movement. The parishes which have jumped into their neighborhoods and become involved in the problems of their culture have become Spirit-filled churches. They have become places where love has taken on flesh, where the bent have been straightened, and where the broken have been healed. Scores of methods have been used; new tools have come to hand as the work progressed; completely different situations have been confronted and resolved. But in every case the Body of Christ has been *involved*, incarnate in the lives of men.

ATONEMENT

The stable was cold, cold and without comfort; the boyhood of the Christ, even within the Holy Family, was full of misunderstanding—"Wist ye not that I must be about my Father's business?" The ministry in Galilee was increasingly uncomfortable, increasingly subject to rejection and misunderstanding even by the apostles themselves. The final pain loomed up in the Cross, but with full knowledge the man Jesus took it on, drenched even before the first lash upon his back with the blood of the prayer of Gethsemane.

The ultimate involvement of the incarnation was identification with fallen humanity; the greatest suffering was the full taking on of that fallen humanity. Flesh did not easily fit the Word of God.

Flesh was a tight-fitting garment, a binding, straitening garment for deity. Christ took it on in the womb of Mary, but only as he wore it did the full cosmic weight settle upon his shoulders. The co-inherence of humanity and deity was stretched to the point of fracture; only the sovereign will of his Person held it together. It stretched to the breaking point as his cry went up, *"Eloi, Eloi, lama sabachthani?"* But it did not break; he held on, and the consummation of his resurrected flesh sounded forth forever the joy and certainty of union, reconciliation, and redemption.

As the Church acts out the involvement of the incarnation, she too must come to the point of identification with fallen humanity's flesh and blood. Each generation of Christians is subjected to the tearing of the flesh within the Church; each generation bleeds out its Gethsemane; each can gauge the success of its identification by the presence of the echoing cry, "My God! My God! Why hast thou forsaken me?" This is not merely Good Friday preaching; it is truth. It means that one must expect suffering in the *process* of identification. There is nothing easy about the coming together of human beings in the relationship of love. As God clothed the story of the birth of Christ in great beauty, as if we could not bear its stark reality, so does he clothe the passion of love with a forestaste of the fruit and joy of love—the pleasure of friendship, the romance of eros, the warmth of family life, the innocence of the children who are the branches of love.

Yet at the heart of all love upon this fallen planet there is ultimately a sword. When a man and his wife are bound together in holy matrimony and look forward to years of happiness together, those who watch shed a tear, particularly those who have been happily married themselves. They know that if this young couple are to reach the joy of complete union of personality, they will undoubtedly pass through the shadow of pain. If it is hard for a man and woman in love to find co-inherence without pain, even within the Grace of the sacrament of matrimony, is it strange that thrusting forth love to a stranger should be a painful process?

This pain is particularly sharp in the depths of the city, where the Church can become the center of this passion. One cannot find a delinquent child who does not fight the one who tries to minister to him. Psychiatrists tell us that absorbing this hostility is part of the therapeutic process; they are saying, of course, in other language what Christ wrote forth upon the Cross. Underneath the light friendship of the Negro and white man there is often anger, guilt, and pain, which finally, but not without passion, the love of God can set aside. The successful businessman, faced with the enormous responsibility of industry and his own powerlessness to direct it away from the violence it lays upon human personality (including his own), finds reconciliation within his own person a point of pain. Fellow Christians, working together, sharing the same Eucharist, serving the same altar, find demonic forces pulling them apart in petty jealousies and in major differences over tactics in the battle for the Kingdom. A preacher, loving his people and forced by that love to cast forth from the pulpit words that will inevitably divide and hurt and anger, is torn within himself between roles of so-called prophecy and pastoral concern.

Long before we even touch upon the suffering of sharing, we encounter the suffering of the process of unity, the process of atonement. If the Church does not realize this suffering to be part of her vocation, she will falter and retreat on the very threshold of effective redemptive life. The businessman will reject the Church because he cannot agree with the statements of its leadership nor endure this painful disagreement. He does not realize that, whoever is right or wrong, this tension is part of the atoning process. The urban parish timidly beginning its first work with inner-city children may abandon the project when the children express their gratitude in broken windows, foul language, and irreverent behavior. The parish may not recognize this as part of the healing of minds and souls. The well-meaning white "liberal" will throw in the sponge after one good healthy rejection by a Negro acquaintance; the Negro leader will cast off his new-found alliance with a white man when he finds the white man not ready or able to march in a picket line. The young couple will seek other amours after the pain of erotic anger first bursts upon them in its surprising terror, not knowing that dealing with that anger is the way to a depth of unity they never could have imagined.

The Church must *be there* in all areas of the city and its life. The clergy and laymen must combine forces. If possible, the pastor should live next to his parish, submitting himself to the same forces as those faced by his people. The laity from all walks of life must attempt to identify their lives one with the other, expecting the process to be painful, yet in faith, and even more in hope, knowing that joy cometh in the morning.

The passion is not concluded in the act of unity. Once the identification has begun and to some extent been accomplished, there is the additional burden of shared suffering. These "others" whose pains are outside the pain of an individual Christian's body are now part of his body and their pain becomes a part of his pain. His child suffers, and he perhaps sometimes suffers even more than the child in the sympathy of love. If he suffers with his child he gives strength to the child by holding his hand as it squeezes the pain away in the feverish grasp of fingernails. In such a way each Christian is the child of every other Christian; each leans upon and loves the other. St. Anthony, even as a hermit, was able to express it. Each Christian must be a *double man:* "He must suffer, weep, and mourn with him and must be accepted by him as if he himself had actually put on the body of his neighbor, and as if he had acquired his countenance and soul, and he must suffer for him as he would for himself."

Our vocation as the Church in the city is *being there* to share
the great, heaving anguish of the metropolis.

RESURRECTION AND LIFE IN THE KINGDOM

"A man cannot step into the same stream." In saying this,
Heraclitus knew that the stream is always changing. One could
say "A man cannot live in the same city" for similar reasons.
Moreover, the same city is a different city for each inhabitant as
he looks upon it with a different eye, peering forth from a different soul, carried in a different body. It is inaccurate, then, to generalize about a city in terms of the life and salvation of its people.

I remember so well the distaste with which I first viewed
Jersey City. To me, an outsider, it was ugly, formless, dirty, and
gray. Eight years later, on leaving Jersey City, I was leaving my
home—a city where I had known great happiness, where my
closest friends still lived, and where I had been honored to share
birth, life, and death with our people. It had become a warm
place, a friendly place, a place of beauty—beauty not of buildings but of lives, of courage, of love, and of faith. There was incredible beauty of hope, beauty of the face of youth and of the
face of age, beauty of laughter and of tears, and the beauty of
Christ walking among his poor. "A man cannot live in the same
city."

The incarnation and atonement are not ends in themselves,
but means toward the resurrected life in the Kingdom of God.
The resurrection of Jesus shone forth from his risen body, but
even this was not so important as the risen joy of the fellowship
with him. Some day we may know a risen body, but the Kingdom as it now exists around us is one of redeemed relationships.
To live in the Kingdom is to live the risen life of love in the
presence of the Spirit. In involvement and identification is this
risen life begun.

It is strange that despite the horror with which cities have been described down through the ages the vision of the heavenly Jerusalem has never lost its glow. No hymns resound more firmly from the heart of a congregation than "Jerusalem the golden" or "Jerusalem, my happy home." The Bible considers the City as the ultimate symbol of the Kingdom, for it is man's fellowship with other men which forms the Communion of Saints in which they are united to the Trinity.

". . . [Abraham] looked for a city which hath foundations, whose builder and maker is God" (Hebrews 11:10).

"And I John saw the holy city, the new Jerusalem coming down from God out of heaven, prepared as a bride adorned for her husband. . . . And God shall wipe away all tears from their eyes; and there shall be no more death, neither sorrow, nor crying, neither shall there be any more pain: for the former things and passed away" (Revelation 21:2,4).

Accompanying the vision of the heavenly City in the pages of the Bible is the nightmare of the demonic city. Many of the Bible's cities have become symbols of the perversion of relationship, the twisting of the love proper to the holy City. Babylon, the great mother of harlots, depicts Rome, soon to rival Jerusalem herself as a symbol of the holy City; yet she is described as the epitome of harlotry, the commercialization of love become lust. There are Sodom, synonymous with perversion, and Jericho, which stood in the way of the Kingdom. Later, the city symbolism was taken up by St. Augustine, who used it to lay a foundation for the culture of a thousand years.

Cities are symbols of the life of a nation. Paris tells us more of Frenchmen than the word France; London contains the steady ponderousness, the reliable strength, the northern beauty of all that is English. Athens *is* Greece. These "symbol cities" represent not only the virtue of the culture. They also speak of another aspect: Montmartre, Soho, London docks, Times Square, or San

Francisco's Chinatown. Each has its special Babylon living and inseparably intermixed with the bit of God's Kingdom therein. As Augustine said, "For the two cities [of the predestinate and the reprobate] are in the world confused together and conmixed, until the general judgment make a separation." [1]

What has been said about cities could, of course, be said about human life in general. But it is in the intense, nervous life of the city that the evidences of these things are more clear and where the Church needs the more clearly to see them. There is a redeemed city. Again, as Anthony the Hermit said, "Your life and your death are with your neighbor." There *is* a redeemed City—the atoning, co-inhering city—where broken relationships are redeemed and made holy by the exchange of burdens, as Charles Williams points out in *The Image of the City*. The exchange of burdens ranges between the most intimate exchange of marriage, the ultimate exchange of the Eucharist, and the most casual exchange of doing a favor for an acquaintance. Williams describes the city in terms of the last paragraph of the Apostles' Creed:

The Holy Ghost is its life, the Holy Catholic Church its name here; the Communion of Saints the continuing co-inherence; Forgiveness of sins, the redeeming of broken interchange by deeper interchange; the Resurrection of the Body, the glory of the Holy Flesh by which so much is known . . . the Life everlasting, infinite power in all its glory.

This thinking about the holy City speaks to two aspects of the life of the urban church, its inner life and its relation to the city around it. There must be a conscious effort on the part of the staff and most involved members of the urban parish to act out the principles of the Kingdom in Christian community, about which so much is now being written. Such community gives the

[1] *The City of God*, I:34.

Holy Spirit a group through which to guide his efforts. Community makes a place to which the cold of body, heart, mind, or soul may come for warmth. It also provides a place in which those who must shoulder the endless burden of the parish may find mutual support and the warmth of human love, through which the love divine must reach them. There must be an effort to see the City around the parish as a place of the Kingdom too, to feel not that "they" are out there and "we" are in here, but to know that perhaps unknowingly there are many "outside" living the redeeming life closer to the heart of Christ than any within the formal Church. Christians must search humbly for the Kingdom around them, seek it, uncover it, find it, and join forces with it; thus the united City may shine in greater brilliance.

This truth can be expressed in another way. The heavenly City on earth, the Kingdom of God, is not coterminous with the institutional Church. The purpose of the institutional Church is not to "snatch brands from the burning" or to take souls out of the wicked environment of the city into the saving environment of the parish. In the first place, the life of the parish may not be a saving life at all; it may be a place of evil, gossip, and prejudice. Secondly, as we have seen, there is much of the Kingdom outside the institutional Church, and it would be presumptuous to infer otherwise. Thirdly, the purpose of the Word made Flesh is to redeem the world rather than to redeem individuals *from* the world. Thus as each person is made a member of the Body of Christ, or made conscious of the meaning of that membership, he is sent forth into the world to be a leaven or to be the salt of the earth. He is to go forth not presumptuously, but humbly, knowing that he will find Christ there before him—in prison, in a hospital, in the face of the suffering, in the Magdalene love found even in a brothel. He will find Christ out there, far beyond the walls of the parish, and he will rejoice to meet him.

There will be a coming together of this member of Christ with the presence of Christ, and the coming together will be joyous.

There is a crying need for a Christian ideology, as Bishop Ted Wickham is continually saying, one which will rival the ideology of the Communist. But it is not yet worked out. This ideology cannot be worked out in a vacuum; this must be done by those who are living in the city, experiencing the tension of cities. They must hammer out of the daily revelation of this life the new insights into God's Providence.

CONCLUSION

We could continue to discuss the whole spectrum of Christian theology in the light of modern metropolitan life. Our purpose has been to touch upon a few theological ideas to show that properly understanding them is absolutely essential to the work of the Church in the city. Without this understanding the Church's work can become secular and institutionalized; it can become self-centered and exclusive; it can become concerned only with the peace and well-being of man on the most superficial level. However, with a continual theological frame of reference, we can sense the work of the Holy Spirit in giving understanding and guidance so that the methods will become clear as the work continues. Finally, it must be recognized that the work of the Church in the inner city may be a failure in any worldly terms, perhaps even in superficial spiritual terms. But unless the Church is willing to sustain these failures, which often have within them the seeds of Calvary, she may find herself empty of the resurrection life.

5. Urban Spirituality

"During the reign of Diocletian, St. Antony, the first of the Christian hermits, took up his dwelling between the Nile and the Red Sea. Alone, ascetic, emaciated, he gave to the Church the same formula: 'Your life and your death are with your neighbor.'"

—CHARLES WILLIAMS

AT A recent conference on the urban ministry, a young man who had been silent for several sessions rose to his feet and delivered an impassioned speech, pleading for more emphasis on the spiritual life in our thinking. Those of us who were leading the conference were surprised and perhaps a little hurt that he thought we underestimated the importance of prayer. We had taken for granted that everything we said about the work of the Church in the city *must* be based on a vigorous relationship with our Lord. But lest readers of this book have a similar misunderstanding, let us consider some examples which illustrate the kinds of problems and opportunities peculiar to the devotional life of a Christian in the modern city.

If we think of God's Grace as coming into the world with a great downward sweeping movement, described in the theological terms of creation, incarnation, and redemption, the local Christian community would be one of the channels through which this flow of God's power could occur. But this is the very place where the Grace of God is too often blocked, twisted beyond recognition, or at best squeezed into a trickle. In the brief historical review of the previous chapter, one pattern was clear: the great times of the Church's life have come to pass when the Holy Spirit broke through into the world in new patterns through the sensitivity and response of an individual or a small group. Such a breakthrough does not "just happen" unless the Christians involved are open to the movement of the Spirit— alive, alert, flexible, and unafraid to respond to his bidding. This means individuals on their knees, and it means Christian community, corporate life together in the Spirit. When we are strong the Spirit guides and gives courage; when we are weak he heals and strengthens and comforts. The city man, living with a special intensity, needs such strength and guidance more than most.

This chapter is written for both clergy and laymen. One of the deepest problems of today's Church is a redefining of the lay ministry. We clergy are waking up to the fact that the laity are fellow workers, rather than glorified servants on the one hand or employers and salary-payers on the other. They are not just pupils and clients and patients, but ministers of God who have a clear and special work to do which the clergy cannot do. One of the causes of the downgrading of the laity lies in the fact that their spiritual life has often been thought of in different terms than the spiritual life of the clergy. Books are published about the devotional life of the priest; they are full of red meat and stiff ascetical theology. Books on the devotional life of the layman seem full of thin milk and sentimentality; the author struggles so to make the subject interesting and avoids theology so scrupulously that he has little time for communicating the stuff of the life of prayer. The result is a sort of spiritual snobbishness on the part of the clergy and spiritual inferiority complexes on the part of the laity.

Those laymen who do develop a strong life of prayer do it with considerable effort against the tide of custom. They risk being thought strange; they risk using the wrong words in front of knowledgeable clergy; they risk trying to jump the fence and becoming imitation clergy, "sacristy rats." We must insist that lay Christians have the same urgent demands upon them in terms of prayer and study as do the clergy, and that prayer is prayer with or without a collar back to front. Thus in this chapter, I shall not separate the one from the other, but start with the hypothesis that both are Christians, period.

ON LEARNING TO PRAY

Concepts of learning to pray vary between two extremes. One view is that prayer is so natural a thing for a man to do and so individual and private a thing that "instruction" is unnecessary. Or, on the other hand, that it is a complicated esoteric discipline, far removed from life as most people know it; it must be learned from scratch, like water skiing. An analogy more useful would be to compare it to running. Anyone can run, but a champion runner needs instruction and intense discipline. Although instruction and life-long discipline are required, the various aspects of the life of prayer in their beginnings issue very simply from the natural praying of the average churchgoer. The instinct for some kind of daily prayer becomes a habit. Meditation issues out of the occasional stopping in a quiet church which most church people do from time to time, especially when they have a problem too heavy to bear. The so-called practice of the presence of God is an intensification of the occasional realization we all have, even in the middle of a busy day, that somehow God is around and concerned with our daily lives. The Eucharistic life is a deeper understanding of going to church on Sunday; intercession and the Christian community are clarified as we better understand whatever part of being a Christian lies beyond our own personal and private religion. Deepening the life of prayer, then, means the development of these sometimes crude instincts into a state of what Martin Thornton calls *proficiency* (Martin Thornton, *Christian Proficiency*).

We can begin, as Julian of Norwich points out, with a reverent wonder at God in his creation, found in as simple an object as a hazel nut; we can continue from there, step by step, to the vision of God in all his glory. The path is long and sometimes arduous. It is up to the Christian to keep strong his effort, so that the door to his soul will be open to the work of God. Be prepared for boredom, perhaps long stretches of boredom; be prepared for discouragement; be prepared for restlessness and a sense of meaninglessness; be prepared for the feeling that the Bible and Christian literature seem a far, far cry from the days of your life. But be assured that every bit of effort is worthwhile, and be assured that the ways of worship worked out by the Church over the years are tried and true and with a little imagination can carry you along in the most complex and trying times. This life, however, must be sought as a total thing; it cannot be relegated to Sunday morning or departmentalized as "religion."

Few people have the imagination to provide for themselves a varied diet for the daily prayer they need. As the tensions of city life drain the human spirit of imagination and psychic energy, little is left at the end of the day (or at the beginning, for that matter) for the kind of work necessary to provide such variation. The use of such a liturgical volume as the Book of Common Prayer results not only in rich variety but in an additional and far more important realization: one is not alone, he is not just choosing a useful spiritual pastime, for stretching across the city and across the world is the Church, praying with him, offering to God the Father the love of the Body of his Son. This is being part of the cosmic life of the Trinity; it is participating in the infinite power and strength of almighty God himself and being a citizen of the City, the heavenly Jerusalem. In all the uncertainty and confusion of being a Christian living in a modern metropolis, one can be assured that this much of life is solid and true. Such daily prayer is the staple of his diet. It is something he offers as a work, the *opus dei*, and it makes no difference whether he enjoys it or not, whether he feels God's presence or not. It is something to be done.

Strangely enough, for example, coming to the point of saying the daily offices is often a turning point in the spiritual life of one who uses the Book of Common Prayer. I have worked with several persons who up to that time were attracted to a more serious life of prayer, but still were nibbling around the edges, subject to enthusiasms and lagging times, looking for emotion, a sense of wonder, or a sense of peace. When they finally (reluctantly) took on the obligation of the offices they suddenly matured and found themselves on solid ground. They started with just the Psalm as a daily rule and gradually filled out the lessons and the prayers. Finally, the Prayer Book offices are so arranged that the important parts of Scripture are read through each year, so that one gains a balanced intake of the Word of God while fulfilling the obligation of praise. The recitation of the office, then, can become the backbone of the daily life of prayer.

There are other most important kinds of prayer as well, each of which has its particular function. At least an average of ten minutes each day (and hopefully longer as one moves along) should be given to informal prayer or "meditation." This is the equivalent of casual conversation with a friend, sharing of problems, or sitting quietly beside one you love. It is a time when the human spirit attempts to be quiet and listen to God, who can communicate in the silence. This communication does not ordinarily come in a "voice" or a "vision," but in the moving of one's thoughts. Various techniques to assist this process have been developed by masters of the prayer life. These can be found in such spiritual classics as *The Introduction to the Devout Life* of St. Francis de Sales, *The Spiritual Exercises* of St. Ignatius Loyola, *Self-abandonment to Divine Providence* of de Caussade, and countless others, as well as in modern writings on the subject like *School of Prayer*, by Olive Wyon, and *Christian Proficiency*, by Martin Thornton. But all the techniques come down to the simple and yet complex process of spending a few minutes quietly alone with God each day, when you are trying to "hear" him, rather than trying to speak to him.

One most important aspect of informal prayer is coming to know the Person of Jesus Christ in the atmosphere not of study but of prayer. To this end, an easy way is to take one of the Gospels and read a verse or two which catches your interest, or a scene from the Gospel, or a parable. Picture it, think about it, feel about it, understand it, and sense the trait in Jesus' character which is shown forth within it. Then take this new insight into the Person of Christ directly into your own life as you are living it day by day in the city. You need it. A conscientious clergyman or layman is continually weighed down by other people's problems. Sometimes it is hard to be patient, sometimes the very burden of complex relationships in city life is overpowering.

One morning when I was feeling this way, I happened to be using as a subject for meditation one of my favorite stories about our Lord, the one in which the paralytic is let down through the roof (Mark 2) that Jesus might heal him. This spoke to me "loud and clear." Jesus was not irritated at this fantastic imposition upon him, when he was already so overwhelmed by demands that he was cornered and set upon. I am sure he was tempted to resent this additional crisis, as you and I resent the extra transient stopping us on our way home after a grueling day. And yet there was not a hint of resentment, rather a clear strong statement of healing love, which Jesus could not have summoned as a human being, but which he must have summoned, as it were, from the depths of his divine nature. You and I have this same strength available to us if we are in close relationship to him. Obvious? Of course. And yet, although I had read the story a hundred times before, I had not "emotionally accepted" it, as the psychiatrists say, until I had prayed through this scene from the Gospel and found it speaking exactly to one of the most recurrent problems of the Christian in the modern city.

Thus informal prayer is an indispensable way of bringing the person of Jesus immediately into the rough and tumble of city life and of enlivening the spiritual life of the individual, the parish, and the Church. As one works along through the Gospels, the vastly different setting in which Jesus moved ceases to seem so vastly different; and the time of prayer seeks ever deeper levels, sometimes beyond words, sometimes of naked confrontation in the silence. Setting aside the ten minutes or more is the greatest problem of all. It can only be done by establishing a strong and regular habit, making an appointment with God, as it were, each day, at the beginning of the day if possible. This may involve stopping at a church on the way to work or getting up ten minutes earlier each morning. But it will soon become clear that such a procedure is one's growing edge of development as a Christian.

PRACTICING THE PRESENCE OF GOD

The natural sequel to daily informal prayer is more frequent realization of God's presence during the day. One brings along a memory of the Gospel scene, a phrase that came to life, a resolution made in his presence, or perhaps just a sense of God's nearness. In this way our Lord penetrates the life of the city. Thus does he penetrate that part of life which is lived during the week away from church. Now it is not easy to sense Christ's immediacy as one conducts the daily affairs of life, but it is an absolutely necessary sensitivity, because he is there, whether one senses him or not. As meditation is, in part, an attempt to project ourselves into the space and time of the historical Jesus, so the practice of the presence of God, recollection, is an attempt to realize his presence in the space and time which we inhabit.

The ethical problems faced every day by men and women in business, or for that matter by any man or woman in his community life, are complex. The solution to one's action in the midst of complexity is not to evade thinking of the action in Christian terms (as most people do) but rather to work out the "lesser of two evils" and to realize that the lesser of two evils is "the good," the greatest good available under the circumstances. This little excursion into moral theology has a purpose, for without some understanding of Christian ethics, of the grays as well as the blacks and the whites of life, the practice of the presence of God in metropolitan life would be a well-nigh impossible strain. As we think of building the City of God, it seems that our minimum aim must be at least to have the Christian view presented in each situation, at least have it *one* of the considerations along with, let us say, sales, labor, and production in the decision. The courage and wisdom for such penetration comes, for the most part, through the intensity of the individual's conviction and his nearness to the mind of Christ—his openness to the guidance of the Spirit. This in turn comes from his life of prayer. Our Lord's surprising insights, his ability to cut through to the heart of extremely difficult questions, did not come from intellectual agility, but from a complete knowledge of the will of his Father.

The practice of the presence of God is an end in itself and ultimately more important than any of the ethical by-products mentioned above; the end and purpose of the Christian life is worship, closeness to God. However, in the same way that this "spiritual" exercise has its ethical results and is bound inextrica-

bly with daily life, so are ethical and moral actions full of devotional content. One of the misconceptions of the Christian life is
that you store up spiritual power through prayer in order that
you may have the strength to do the difficult Christian works
which are laid before you. There is some truth in this idea. But
the great saints and the effective Christians, those people who
really communicate the light, are those who find strength *in* the
doing of the work of Christ and through their loving actions find
new power for prayer. The principle at work here is expressed
in the simple and familiar words of Jesus, "Thou shalt love the
Lord thy God with all thy heart and strength and mind, and the
second [commandment] is *like* unto it, Thou shalt love thy
neighbor as thyself." In other words, you meet Christ himself
in others, and you find him in the tensions of daily life.

St. Francis had to use the most violent will power to make
himself clasp the cold leper to himself, but, in so doing, he found
that the leper wore the face of Christ. This is the magic of true
charity, not an unwilling sense of duty which communicates distaste to the person ministered to, but an upside-down radical
love which somehow loves the unlovable even more than the lovable because our Lord dwells more intensely within the unlovable. That upside-down kind of value finds deep joy in the
most tearing of situations because they are part of the crucifixion,
still being acted out in the Body of Christ, the Church. Thus,
dealing with difficult or even repulsive persons can be and is a
sacramental meeting with Christ because he is in them and also
because the love for the unlovable is a love which seeks no return
for loving and is therefore most like Christ's own love. Thus, dealing with one's enemies in a spirit of forgiveness and love is a resurrection experience because it partakes of the Cross. The Christian life, then, is the constant flowing of love from God to us, to
our friends, to strangers, to "enemies," and back again—love,

suffering, forgiveness, joy—shaking us down as it were into an identity with him who lived and loved and forgave and suffered and still does within and through his Church. This, not sterile moralism; this, not quiet pietism; this, not emotional repetitive conversions, is the stuff of the Christian life.

CORPORATE PRAYER

Within both Protestant and Roman Catholic circles there has been a great revival of Bible study in the group context. Perhaps it is the greatest return to Scripture since the Reformation. Some feel that the key to the problems of the reunion of Christendom will be found through this use of the Bible. In any case, whether it be through Bible study, through prayer groups of various kinds, through "cells" with various purposes, it is absolutely essential that every Christian have part of his devotional life in the rather intimate corporate life of a small community. There is a flow of the Spirit that is liberated when two or three are gathered together which seems different from that within the individual prayer life. The Pentecostal experience of the apostles is the touchstone for this part of the work of the Spirit.

One can see the validity of the Spirit in the vigor which almost always comes out of a true corporate experience. Parish life conferences have changed the life of many congregations; Bible study groups have been the means of altering the direction of parishes; many men and women have first found God through participation in a prayer group; the record of Alcoholics Anonymous needs no elaboration. This is not the place to describe the techniques of such group life. One can say firmly that this kind of intimate group life is more necessary in an urban parish than perhaps anywhere else, because the uncertainty of our direction in the modern city can only be rightly clarified by the guidance of the Spirit. The problems are too immense; there are too many unknowns to be solved by the human mind unaided. Nor are there models to follow. We must rely on the Spirit.

The importance of corporate worship to the individual in his life of prayer and as the ultimate setting for the spiritual life of the parish cannot be overemphasized. As in private prayer there should be a balance between the use of form and informality; so in corporate religious expression there should be a balance between spontaneous and flexible spirituality (Bible groups, prayer cells, etc.) and liturgical life. The liturgy among other things expresses the given, ongoing life of the Church, the Body of Christ in visible action. By continually being part of this, especially in the Eucharist, one is brought back repeatedly to the norm of Christianity; he finds the pattern and the power of God's action. Sunday by Sunday, this Eucharistic action takes place all over the world; this is the beating heart of the Church. Into this action the individual pours all that is his, all that he has done, all that he is; and from the Eucharist he takes forth the strength of the Risen Body of our Lord. All individual prayer life points toward this Holy Communion and issues from it. If seen clearly as it is, the Eucharist provides a sure cure for religious fads, self-centered religiosity, and introverted parochialism. The Eucharist shows again and again that we are dependent on God's action, not he on ours. Thus the tired and discouraged, the tense and upset, and the distracted and doubting can come, take part in the Lord's Supper, and know that God does all that is necessary for them, even when they are lost in the city of men and can do nothing for themselves.

MINISTRY OF THE LAITY

This seems an appropriate place to add some thoughts on the so-called ministry of the laity. I bypass the obvious lay ministry already being carried out effectively in most parishes, that of keeping the institution of the Church going, that of teaching, service, and money-raising. These are essential roles and not to be belittled; however, they do not present a problem, for the laity understand their responsibility here.

Other slightly less obvious fields of the lay ministry which are being developed continually are: lay evangelism, calling by lay people on new members and the shut-ins, and prayer and Bible study groups, as ends in themselves and sometimes as means to action. There is the pastoral ministry of many laymen, carried out quietly and effectively; every priest knows of two or three people in his parish who are discreet, wise, and loving, to whom he can turn over someone in trouble for a little extra friendship during a bad time, people who on their own take responsibility for others. There is also the ministry of morale, of those who invigorate vestry meetings, by their very enthusiasm carrying along the fearful and negative members of the parish family, and of those who minister to the rector, who bolster his sagging spirits, standing behind him loyally but also telling him frankly where he is wrong in the privacy of their own relationship. These and many other lay ministries are carried on within the context of parish life. But now I would like to look a little more deeply into the ministry of the layman *outside* the parish structure.

One definition of a layman is a "competent Christian with a special vocation of a nonclerical nature." The Church infiltrates the "world," involving the gospel and its values in our culture, whether it be in the intellectual life of the university, the political life of the city, or the leadership of industry (which shapes our civilization more than any other institution); in this infiltration the laity must be the minister. For they are the only ones with competence in the field concerned. Let us say that the gospel insists on justice in the personnel policy of industry. Can

the untrained clergyman work out the complications of wages
and profits, of night and day shifts, of the overpressuring of
management personnel, or of the diminution of the social ills
described in W. H. Whyte's *Organization Man?* No priest as
such can begin to venture into this realm. It is the layman and
he alone who knows and *respects* the discipline of his calling
enough to translate the gospel into its life. The clergy's role is
to inspire and make training available.

But this is easier said than done, for this is an extremely
"touchy" area. Some feel that the Church should stay within her
neo-Gothic walls, but even with those of whatever political view
who feel the Church should speak to the "world" there are still
difficulties. The clergy often do nothing because they rightly feel
incompetent in the field of such secular disciplines as medicine
and ditch digging. The laity hang back because they are uncertain about the Christian ethic, often feeling guilty about those
things which actually are not sinful or perhaps over which they
cannot have control, while neglecting the very areas where perhaps they could bring to bear the justice of the Kingdom.

A CHRISTIAN IDEOLOGY

What is needed, it seems to me, is a three-way dialogue:
clergy-layman-world. In such a dialogue continuing over the
months or even years the *joint* disciplines of theology and secular
vocation can interchange and inform each other, bringing forth
a synthesis, a Christian *ideology* which can be the tool of confident laymen proudly carrying on their ministry in the world.

The dynamic for this ideology would come from the religious
life of the parish and the individuals within it *caring enough* to
undertake this new phase of life. This means, for most parishes,
a more intense sense of the Spirit, a deeper interchange of love,
a more inclusive membership, and above all a strong Eucharistic

life. The Holy Communion furnishes the pattern and the power for all phases of the Christian life and contains within itself the solutions to all aspects of man's life with God and with other men.

The substance of this ideology would be found in the reviewing of the principles of theology *as they apply to specific problems* in the life of the laity concerned. I speak of such principles as *personhood,* its relation to the impersonalization of such diverse disciplines as medicine and industry; *creation,* how man is co-creator with God and how even the most demonic of twentieth-century creations must have in them the image of God and therefore can in some way be redeemed; *Christly charity,* the Sermon on the Mount and its relation to social welfare, private or public; *Church and State,* and its implications for the whole "Christ and Caesar" problem. One could go on indefinitely. However, each group of "dialoguists" under the guidance of the Spirit will forge out the areas of greatest need for its place in the scheme of divine Providence.

Let us not wait for the national headquarters of a denomination to send out a program. People there are not magicians. Start where you are; do not procrastinate and say, "Let George do it, and when he does we will grudgingly follow." Knowledge will not necessarily come from there, and if it does there remains the problem of how to teach and motivate. But local Christians acquiring the knowledge for themselves have the most effective way of teaching and of motivation. Bishop Wickham, who has led the highly creative and successful Industrial Mission in Sheffield, England, has developed the kind of thing we are discussing. He is fond of saying that "if you look deeply enough into any human problem, you find God." As we have mentioned earlier, Julian of Norwich said this long ago about looking into a hazel nut and finding him. One can also find God, surprisingly enough, in a nasty wage-hour controversy or the policy discussion of a group of doctors on the prolonged terminal illnesses of old people.

Laymen thus taught by themselves and thus motivated can go forth with power so that the councils in which they participate (university faculty meeting, board of directors meeting, or whatever) will have—as at least *one* of the values involved in any deep decision—the Christian value. This is the lay ministry par excellence; it is fulfilling the Christian vocation in the secular job whatever it may be. This frees the clergy from amateurishness in areas for which they are not qualified, and relieves the nagging guilt and malaise on the part of the conscientious layman that somehow being a vestryman cannot be the main function of his life as a Christian. Now I do not wish to infer that all this is a brand new idea; every Christian always takes his value structure and lovingness with him wherever he goes and often wrestles conscientiously over very difficult ethical problems. But there must be a more intense, conscious, corporate effort in this direction so that such struggles with conscience are not solitary.

To summarize, then. We look at the lay ministry as *primarily* the work of the Christian on the job for which he gives the best of himself, whatever that job may be. We look to the church as the place where he can find instruction and power to carry out this ministry and find the strength he needs for his personal and family life. His secondary vocation is to help the institutional church in whatever way he can function best, whether on the governing board or teaching Sunday School. We are living in urgent times. The Church still seems to some people irrelevant to the culture in which we live; our cities, our schools, our jobs, our foreign policy are only very slightly affected by the Church. Christians as a result find themselves under pressure, torn between making a living or even surviving and being a Christian. We must begin somewhere to influence the world around us, rather than being tossed about by economic and sociological forces, as the Marxists claim to be inevitable. And there is no way to exercise such influence without beginning where we are, working out an ideology, a penetration, an involvement in the surrounding world.

6. The Church, the City, and the Word

"To think of the pattern is not to be part of the pattern; to talk of exchange is not to exchange."

—CHARLES WILLIAMS

IT IS eleven-thirty on Sunday morning. The preacher kneels during the sermon hymn. It is the last moment before God is to use this man for the delivery of his Word to the people of his Church and to the world around them. No matter how often it occurs, week after week, year after year, this is a moment of truth, of deep excitement. The preacher empties himself, calls upon the Holy Spirit, thinks for the last time what the principal thrust of the sermon is to be—compassion, judgment, sacrifice, or power. He arises, walks slowly to the pulpit, and arranges his notes. The music stops and he sees his people, faces upturned to the silence. "In the name of the Father, and of the Son, and of the Holy Ghost . . ." he begins to preach.

Into this moment goes not only the time of preparation of this sermon, but his whole life up to now, and into the hearing of the Word goes the whole life of the people who listen. The effectiveness of his preaching, therefore, depends on factors far beyond technique and the content of the notes which lie before him.

The Episcopal Church, like some other liturgical churches, has tended to underestimate the importance of preaching; her clergy, by emphasizing the liturgy, often unconsciously have excused themselves from the difficult discipline of sermon preparation. Furthermore, the new emphasis on small group Bible study, the importance of "weekday" Christianity, family services, the widening of parish activity which looms so large as an administrative task for the clergy, the new interest in skilled counseling: these and other useful modern ideas have little by little cut the ground from under good preaching.

Urban parishes have their own problems of pulpit communication. The congregation may be lacking in formal education; its background may be so different from that of the preacher that communication of ideas, as well as words, is tricky. Or, as in many downtown parishes, the congregation may be so varied that it is well-nigh impossible to reach a happy medium at which the college professor is not bored and the day laborer understands. Despite these obstacles and despite the fact that many persons belittle the efficacy of the sermon, it is still an essential part of the Church's life. It is the sacrament of the Word. It is not supposed to be "educational" in the sense of communicating information, but "inspirational" in the literal sense—a means of encouraging the work of the Holy Spirit. It is a way of bringing to life the Word which lies buried within the words of Scripture. At the very least, preaching is an opportunity to have the attention of a great many people in an atmosphere of reverence. The preacher has a deep responsibility to be a careful steward of these moments.

First, we will make a few comments about the preacher as pastor, priest, and prophet; then will follow a discussion of the acting out of the Word, without which preaching is merely pleasant or unpleasant entertainment. Finally, we will deal with the special problem of the spreading of the Word through the fragmented islands of metropolitan life.

THE PREACHER AS PASTOR

Passages in the Bible which seem to release the prophet from the responsibility of whether the people hear or reject his message can be bothersome.

And they, whether they will hear, or whether they will forbear . . . yet shall know that there hath been a prophet among them. And thou, son of man, be not afraid of them, neither be afraid of their words, though briers and thorns be with thee, and thou dost dwell among scorpions: be not afraid of their words, nor be dismayed at their looks, though they be a rebellious house (Ezekiel 2:5-6).

Ultimately, it is true, no one can *make* another listen. Yet for the prophet of the New Covenant, is it enough to sound off in anger (which sometimes is one's own anger and not the anger of Jahweh) and let the chips fall where they may? This may be permissible for the wandering prophet, but it cannot be so for us who are charged with pastoral responsibility. In this time of deep fear and conflict in the American scene, perhaps the most agonizing problem of the pulpit is this conflict between the prophetic and the pastoral ministries. One patiently builds the pastoral relationship week after week and then feels obliged to tear it down with a scorching sermon on "Race Relations Sunday"! Is there no way out of this dilemma?

One cannot retreat from the obligation of God's love expressed in his judgment, nor from the obligation of that love as expressed in healing tenderness. The only way open seems to be the continual expression of both, even though their tension in the heart of the pastor sometimes feels mighty like the Cross. Strangely, this very tension gives life and depth to the preaching of the passion, which is itself at the heart of the Word made flesh.

One tendency in downtown preaching is to overemphasize the prophetic. The preacher is sensitive to his position as the means through which the Word of God is spoken to the city and its culture. Yet the chances are that the majority of those who hear him are at the end of their active lives. Many of them are broken already in the harsh conflicts of the city; many of them need not judgment (they have had that), but the promise of redemption, the assurance of the healing power of Jesus. Over the years the preacher must make certain that they see in him the steady, ongoing concern of the shepherd. Thus, again and again sermons must be taken from the pastoral ministry, especially in large congregations where only a small percentage of the people ever find themselves in a one-to-one conversation with the pastor. Preaching must be a kind of *substitute* for the intimate relationship of the small informal parish.

Insofar as the preacher identifies with the problems he actually finds in pastoral counseling, sooner or later each person will feel "he knows me" and sense, therefore, that "God knows me," for it is in his name that the preaching is done. Having the patience and courage to stay on in a parish, keeping his people in his prayers, being willing to be insulted and misunderstood and still stretch out the hand of reconciliation: these things will deepen the trust. The ears of more and more will be softened, and it will be understood that even the most searing sermons are ministered in love and not hostility, spoken within the context of the deepest of pastoral relationships.

THE PREACHER AS PRIEST

The pastor mediates the love of God; the priest mediates the mystery of God. As the pastor attempts to give the *feeling* of the warmth of God's personal concern, so the priest attempts to communicate the *excitement* of the life of worship. In the pulpit and in front of the altar the priest must bring his people to sense the *mysterium tremendum*. Most congregations are familiar with the devices of the instructed Eucharist, the dialogue sermon, and the need for continual instruction in their part in the service and preparation for it. But all this is useless if the people do not sense the *importance* of what is done in the feeling tone of the total liturgical action.

As the preaching of the pastor depends upon his genuine love for his people as individuals with heavy burdens, so the preaching of the priest depends upon his own involvement in the priestly action. Does he sense the shattering power of the tiny white host? Do his own hands from time to time tremble at its touch? Does he see before him on the altar the hands of Christ strangely mirrored in these most familiar fingers? Does he also sense those hands to be the hands of Judas? Do the great surging waves of the liturgical year break over him in sorrow, in joy, in expectancy, in failure, in victory, and in inner power? The proper preaching of the liturgy must be the communication of these feelings—some of which, sooner or later, every member of the congregation can appropriate for his own devotional life. Thus, of the priest is demanded a careful life of prayer by which his own soul is made sensitive to the presence of Christ, so that he may point it out: "There he is; look at him in all his glory. There he is upon the altar. You can go up and see, and touch, and be made into his glorious Body."

As these things happen, the City is being built within the city; the heavenly Jerusalem exists in some measure within the discouragement and confusion of the metropolis or the parish within it. This, of course, is *most* important in our large depersonalized parishes, where there is so little opportunity for the communicating of the Person of Christ through long and deep conversation. Our people must be brought as quickly as possible to see and know him themselves—to exercise their own priesthood, if you will.

Furthermore, liturgical preaching and liturgical communication are necessary if Christians are to find purpose within the swirl of purposelessness around them. Only through involvement in liturgical action can they find the ultimate purpose of their being—the worship of God. Only through a deep understanding, even if unexpressed, of the Holy Communion can they discern God's presence and work through every aspect of the social process, through every bang and rattle, every fear and loneliness, every harrowing tragedy, or dull gray stretch of time. These circumstances are not God's doing, but God can work to redeem them, as churchmen appropriate the sacramental Grace which he gives his members.

THE PREACHER AS PROPHET

This aspect of the preaching ministry, perhaps more than any other, has been under discussion in recent years, especially among those who occupy the dark pulpits of the inner city. However, a few additional comments are in order on the necessity of the Church speaking to the issues of our day and calling a spade a spade. The intensity of "prophecy" depends upon the existential situation. Sometimes the best prophecy is silence (our friend Ezekiel again). Sometimes one must speak softly and act strongly. Sometimes no action is possible, and so the word must carry the burden of the judgment of God. But preaching must always be related to action. In one downtown parish where the preacher delivered good strong social teaching, the people were perturbed at first. When they found that he never really did anything about it they relaxed, as children with a parent who is continually threatening. His successor arrived and not only began to preach but to act in such areas as integration and neighborhood involvement. He stirred up a hornet's nest. This rector found that it was better not to talk about these matters; rather, he occasionally mentioned how proud he was of the parish's acceptance of responsibility. A rule of thumb for would-be prophets might be: "Do not speak unless you are prepared to act when action becomes possible."

The question under discussion at a recent conference of Cathedral Deans was this: should the preacher mention contemporary problems if he is not an expert in the field? Most of the laymen who were there as advisers from the upper circles of the government said No. One man, a Methodist labor leader, said Yes. The conference agreed with this minority report! The ethical *issues* involved in secular affairs may be pointed out by one with only the background of a morning headline. Solutions are something else again. They should be handled very circumspectly and most often left to the expert laymen. None of us can be an expert on every problem; yet our people, because of our inexpertness, should not be denied the realization that certain real ethical and spiritual problems exist in almost all the major issues of the day.

Often the prophet's role is to go behind the problem to the emotional base at its root—to avoid, for instance, the economic issues of the John Birch platform and deal with the fear which causes the virulence of its method. Perhaps, in the South, he might avoid approving a particular method of integration or its timing and deal with the guilt behind the destruction. Here he would be attempting to bring the healing Word into the areas where redemption can occur, those of confession and forgiveness, of assurance and theological confidence, rather than the areas of politics, sociology, or economics. In other words, the preacher as prophet should deal with that part of each problem in which he is, in a sense, an expert, and deal with it authoritatively and clearly.

BEYOND THE PULPIT

We have noted that what happens in the pulpit at eleven-thirty on Sunday morning has roots in the total life of the preacher and his congregation. It merely articulates the redemptive process which, hopefully, is continuing at all times within the parish, the community, and the world. But one of the things which continues to be a problem is that too often the wrong preachers are preaching to the wrong congregations.

In a parish in a depressed neighborhood, the clergyman is deeply concerned about housing and race relations and can preach effectively on those subjects. Yet his hearers already agree with everything he says. Contrariwise, the suburban preacher probably absorbs some of the philosophy of individual initiative, the worth of economic responsibility to one's own family, etc., and his suburban congregation loves to hear it. However, it is the family in the inner city which, despite its economic problems, should hear this sermon.

It is hard for the suburban preacher, no matter how conscientious he may be, to be passionately concerned over and informed about the very areas in which his congregation needs instruction and, because of their leadership positions in the community, are able to take effective action. If he were vocationally concerned with these things, he would not be in the suburbs. It is hard equally for the inner-city preacher, involved as he is with his people's hardships, to preach firm sermons on stewardship.

Pulpit exchange is probably not the answer, for the congregation can brush off what a visitor says (though he can sometimes do a useful job). Whatever the solution may be, the problem becomes more acute as the "suburban captivity of the Church" intensifies and the barriers between economic classes grow more impenetrable. Noonday preaching could be the answer, but we may as well face the fact that not many people are present except in Holy Week. TV and radio are answers, but this kind of communication is too anonymous to inspire much action. Newspapers help, but in many cities it is hard to "get into" the newspapers. No matter how relevant the Word of God, how can it reach the city?

There seems to be little hope for an answer to the above question within the present structure of the Church. Answers may come as the churches in the city become *the Church* in the city. Answers may come as the units of ministry transcend parish boundaries (for example, the "Sector Plan" in Gibson Winter's book *The Suburban Captivity of the Church*) and as several Christian communities, which may or may not bear the canonical label of parish, share a ministry. Or answers may come in ways not now imagined.

In the meantime, it is up to the clergy of the suburbs to be as well-informed and emotionally involved as possible with the social issues of the city. It is up to the clergy of the inner city to tactfully inform the Church of these issues in many different ways, perhaps through the denominational departments concerned about such matters. Furthermore, it is up to the laymen who live in the suburbs but work in the city to be a part of this continuous communication. If the layman feels the minister is misinformed or biased in preaching on controversial subjects, there is no reason not to say so. If he feels his suburban rector is living on cloud nine, there is no reason for not inviting him downtown for lunch to meet and discuss matters of mutual concern with a group of laymen.

Perhaps the most important point to make is that the laity should realize that the ministry of the Word does not occur in a vacuum; it cannot be preached to a vacuum with any hope of changing lives. This ministry is communication, and communication is a two-way process. Both the laity and the preacher have a responsibility for this ministry. Many clergy have the privilege of having a few constructive laymen who suggest subjects for sermons and give good criticism. This is a delicate situation, for many a good preacher feels possessive of his prerogatives and insists that there be no infringement upon the "freedom of the pulpit." The loyal layman understands this and may feel hesitant to speak. If this barrier and others of hostility and misunderstanding can be broken down, the preaching of the Word can be a lively thing.

The great hope of the communication of the Word which transcends all barriers of education and class is that *the Word will be acted out!* In this action, the noise goes abroad, finds its place in the newspaper, and develops in the dialogue of revelation and response and in the existential conflict of the moment. Although most readers of this book would not agree with the point of view set forth by the preacher, an example of a great series of sermons springing out of social conflict is contained in William Howard Melish's *Strength for Struggle.*

When Ezekiel was struck dumb, he acted out his message; when our Lord wished to demonstrate a truth too deep to be entrusted to words, he enclosed it in an act, often a miracle. Today the modern Babel of voices comes even from the ultimate silence of outer space. It may be that the preaching of the Church once more must be in action and words so descriptive that within them the Word again puts on flesh, to dwell amongst us.

7. The Vocation of the Parish: The Downtown Church

". . . it is never forgotten that the Israelites are members of the nation as the believers are of the Church, and it is the greater organism which is the full subject, at whatever time. Through those greater organisms, as through the many lesser, there arises a sense of corporate mankind. Individuals and companies, and mankind itself, are finally set in relation to that non-human cause and center which is called God."

—CHARLES WILLIAMS

THE most controversial question at many conferences on the urban ministry is whether the parish itself is a completely outmoded institution. Some very responsible participants will say that the quicker we rid ourselves of parishes in the city, the better off we shall be. The author disagrees with this viewpoint most emphatically. The parish is still a viable institution. As one who has spent his whole ministry in urban parishes, he cannot say they are useless: he has seen extraordinary works of redemption going on within them. Some parishes bring a neighborhood alive, are the only source of strength for numbers of people, and provide the only place in a given section of a city where men and women of different races come to know each other as equals.

The parish is still the place where thousands of Christians receive the Holy Communion, humbly and lovingly, week after week.

The controversy would not exist, however, unless there were some very serious problems relating to this institution. One can certainly agree that a parish operated along traditional lines in an urban situation will die quickly. The institution of the parish as we have inherited it is a nineteenth-century organism. It was designed to be effective in a stable and nontransient society based upon the family and supported by a series of conventions and attitudes toward life which the majority of the population accepted and shared. As we have pointed out, this state of affairs hardly prevails in the inner city today.

One can discern a number of specific weaknesses in the parish as it exists today. It is inflexible. Although the statistics are inadequate, one can say safely that 95 per cent of the inner-city parish buildings were erected over forty years ago. In the meantime the city has changed and people have moved. The old neighborhoods no longer exist, and because of the nature of church organization it is almost impossible for a parish to move to another location or to erect another building more suitable for its needs. This inflexibility is due to the *organization* of the parish because those responsible for making the decisions to move or change are leaders working under the parish system. They are the governing boards of laymen who are often psychologically or perhaps financially unable to make radical choices. The decisions may be in the hands of outside leaders who have little understanding of the nature of the inner city or of its importance.

When a parish becomes threatened enough to begin to contemplate a move, the congregation is already on the defensive and will elect defensive leaders. The smaller the parish becomes, the less evangelistic will be its attitude—and the more resistant to change. Thus from the moment trouble begins, a process begins which increases the trouble; the parish is almost like an animal which is caught in the headlights of a train and which stands frozen until the inevitable destruction rolls over it. Some feel that an inner-city parish must die completely before it can hope to be born again into an effective image for the work of its neighborhood. This inflexibility, which increases as the troubles of the parish increase, affects not only the major decision of location but even the less radical decision of whether to minister to the new neighbors, who are usually from a different background.

There is another problem built into the polity of the independent parish. The governing body's primary responsibility is financial, and in a downtown parish men who are financially able are usually elected. However, these men are often extremely conservative by training and have no real understanding of the dynamics of the volatile inner city. They are men of integrity who believe that their main job is to harbor the dwindling resources of the parish treasury. The only alternative to a dying church, in their eyes, is to go to the suburbs where solvency is possible. Criticize this attitude as one will, church laws are often so written that a parish which cannot pay its bills is no longer a parish. Naturally any red-blooded businessman will avoid this kind of seeming defeat.

Of course there are answers to this: the church could remove the stigma of nonparochial status or allow for subsidization without reversion to dependency. An alert Board of Missions or Urban Department which can supervise dependent parishes or missions in a creative way can be another solution. On the other hand, there is a real value in a parish's remaining independent, even when subsidized, and developing the leadership to survive creatively. The diocese, presbytery, or district should work out a flexible system where either can be done, and this presupposes an extremely alert and informed denominational leadership.

What about the clergy? The inner-city parish often has ministers who have become as old and inflexible as the brownstone churches they inhabit. Many cannot get a call elsewhere and therefore have to settle for the slim pay and discouraging life of the pastor of a dying church. They may be neurotic, timid, eccentric, or authoritarian. In recent years city parishes have also drawn many young men who have sensed a missionary vocation in the inner city and have thrown in their lot with this life, seeing it as exciting and far more vocationally satisfying than that in suburbia. Many of these men are magnificent, but they tend to have one thing in common: they are apt to be rather more radical than their lay leaders. Otherwise they would not be there. They are not necessarily radical in political terms, although this is often true; rather, they wish to go to the root of the trouble and minister in unusual, experimental ways. These are good traits, but they run directly counter to the philosophy of most local church boards. Again, the solution comes through more careful supervision from "headquarters." Granted this means more salaried personnel on the department staff, but it also means souls and dollars saved. It is often impossible to find competent persons to carry out this supervision. However, as urban work develops over the years and as effective techniques are learned and adopted, these leadership vacancies should take care of themselves.

Before leaving the administrative level of the inner-city parish, let us note that the problem is not *merely* administrative; it is tinged with deep emotional and spiritual factors. Most of the persons involved, however, are people of good will, and with the proper structure their deep conflicts can be creatively resolved and need not produce the paralysis we often see. The bishop (or his counterpart) and the urban staff must assume the role of "marriage counselor" and build enough flexibility into the situation to offer a variety of solutions. The chief pastor must remove the overwhelming sense of guilt which "failure" entails and communicate a sense of adventure and a pioneer spirit. Help can now be secured from national councils, and the literature on the subject is growing all the time. The churches are in a far better position to deal with the situation than they were a few years ago.

ON BEING THE CHURCH

Perhaps one of the difficulties is a hidden one; we are all subject to stereotyping the local church, to accepting certain things as inevitable, and to allowing habits of thought to stifle the imagination. After all, on one level, the parish is merely a group of Christians functioning under the pastoral care of a clergyman. It usually has an altar with a roof over it, a meeting place, an office from which to conduct corporate business, and a means of relating itself administratively to the denomination at large. If we did not have a parish, it seems we would need at least this much sooner or later. The House Church, the Industrial Mission, the chaplaincy to the institution, and other such structured ministries are valid, but they eventually develop similar organization and are dependent upon the parochial life of the church at large. In thinking through the vocation of the parish let us try to think without stereotypes, allow our imaginations to "brainstorm" the situations which arise, and realize that there is nothing sacred about the way the church is organized beyond the given form of the Holy Catholic Church.

Let us review, for a moment, the special problems of the inner city, or, for that matter, of the metropolis as a whole. The population is mobile and heterogeneous; the living is speeded-up and accompanied by tension and lack of leisure. Senses are dulled, and impersonality prevails in direct relation to density of population. There is "unchurchedness" or even a proletarian distrust of the institutional church. Broken families are frequent; so are economic problems and a higher frequency of "pastoral" problems. Most church materials are inadequate for inner-city work, and there is always frustration and a sense of failure. The Church must address itself to this constellation of traits and at the same time clearly hold in mind the criteria for her ministry.

It is the Church's vocation to be the Church rather than to accomplish certain results; in other words, the Church must try to be itself so definitely that it *looks* like itself, that it *looks* like the Body of Christ. To the Congo nationalist, Lumumba martyred in the jungle looks more like Jesus Christ than does the Archbishop of Canterbury. To the Puerto Ricans of East Harlem, perhaps, Marcantonio looked more like a minister of love than does the pastor of a nearby Fifth Avenue church.

Before we dismiss this by saying "looks deceive," some self-examination is in order. We must see whether the Church really is *involved* and identified with the lives and struggles of the people around its doors, whether it is *loving* to the point of suffering. We must make sure that it is *apostolic*, sent forth into the heart of the city in which it is placed, and that it is *catholic*, inclusive of all the peoples of the city. It must be *holy*, relating itself to God's values as revealed in Jesus Christ rather than to the values of a specific culture. The Church must also be *one*, believing that the faith it professes, if properly expressed, can reach any human being who wishes to receive it. It cannot say, as some churchmen have said, "Leave the inner city to the Fundamentalists and Pentecostals who more readily can minister to the 'non-episcopal' type of people in the inner city."

Once the Church knows what it must be and is aware of some of the special problems facing it in the city, it is then up to each parish to find its particular vocation under God. It is clear that a multitude of factors determine that vocation—the location of the parish, its history, the size of its buildings, and its financial status. The make-up of the congregation, the skills of its clergy, and the direction of the Holy Spirit will have an effect on its work. Each parish needs some sort of periodic self-study, which should be more than a review of the statistics concerning the parish and its community.* The members and their pastor must examine *themselves.*

One method of self-examination could be a series of Bible study groups for the whole parish, centered in such questions as these: What is God's purpose for the world? What is Christ's purpose in the incarnation? What is the purpose of the Church? What is the purpose of the Church in the city? What is the vocation of this parish?

A planning committee can easily find Bible texts which will sharpen the thinking of the people so the Word of God can penetrate their thoughts. After such an exercise, perhaps conducted during Lent, the parish can be re-formed into special interest groups concerning themselves with social relations, education, evangelism, and so forth. If such a self-study program is a deep and honest one, and not something the parish does just to please its clergy, answers will be found. In the process of finding them, the people will be motivated to carry them out.

Hopefully, when this first part of the self-study program has been completed, the special interest groups will wish further information about the parish and the neighborhood before embarking upon overly ambitious plans. The study may be elaborate or simple; there are several alternatives. A good deal of autonomy may be allowed to the special groups (with an occasional meeting of the chairmen and the clergy to make sure that wires are not being crossed), and each group may delve as deeply as it chooses into the area of its concern. After some exploration, or perhaps before breaking into special groups, the

* See Appendix B.

congregation's leaders can re-form to undertake a thorough self-study. The process will not be outlined here since this has been done most effectively in a book, now available in paperback, by one of the best authorities in the field: *Urban Church Planning*, by Walter Kloetzli and Arthur Hillman.

There are dangers in the self-study process which have plagued the church at all levels. If the study is too involved its completion makes the congregation feel that the job is done, and there is little energy left to carry out the plans. The danger of too limited a study is the feeling that *all* the answers have been found. Then, if the first few ventures undertaken are not successful, the cause seems *really* hopeless. Self-study is a tool and a necessary tool, but it is not a substitute for courageous action. No matter what is indicated by graphs and figures, the only final test of the merit of a particular program is to try it and see if it will work. If it does not work, the parish must examine the reasons for its failure.

It is useful to have a planning committee as a permanent parish organization. Having such a committee means that some impartial group which has no ax to grind can keep examining the parish and using imagination without bearing its special organizational interest or the finances of the parish in mind. Furthermore, someone other than the clergyman can submit adventurous programs for consideration. Wonders can be accomplished by changing the roles of laymen and clergy in this regard.

Program planning in urban churches can best be discussed by separate consideration of the downtown church, the inner-city neighborhood parish, and the transitional one. It is as impossible to provide "canned" programs as it is to draw sharp distinctions between the types of parishes. If the suggestion of a possible program for each type seems arbitrary, the ideas included are in many cases interchangeable.

CHARACTERISTICS OF
THE DOWNTOWN CHURCH

The downtown church is located in the very heart of the city, among the offices, entertainment facilities, department stores, and high-rise apartments and hotels. Often it is the "mother church" of the city, and seldom has it lost prestige, even if it is rather weak inside. The congregation is generally a cross section of persons drawn to this old church for a variety of reasons. Its financial structure may be quite solid, its music better than most, and there is probably a tradition of better than average preaching there. The downtown church today is undoubtedly "integrated" to some extent and need not "fear" becoming a parish of one minority group; this just never seems to happen.

The rich variety of its congregation and the breadth of its responsibility makes planning somewhat difficult. For example, an Episcopal church should have *focus* in its program, one major theme in its parish life from year to year, so that people do not become lost in the vague Anglican fog. The variety of need surrounding the downtown church makes such focus seem almost impossible. The fact that it often does occur usually stems from the special interests or talents of its clergy. There is nothing wrong in this per se, so long as the emphasis coincides with the genius of the parish and the clergy do not change so frequently as to confuse or alienate the congregation. These special emphases are especially valid in large metropolitan areas like New York, London, or Chicago. On the other hand, in a small city with only one downtown church, one feels obliged to be all things to all people.

A COMMAND POST

Here is a function which has not been explored fully, but which has occurred here and there because of the chances of finance. Trinity Church, New York, is the classic example of the downtown church with chapels scattered all over town for which it assumes financial responsibility and, to some extent, planning and policy oversight. On a smaller scale, and with looser organizational ties to the smaller parishes, other downtown churches and cathedrals have exercised the same function.

Some downtown churches which are searching for a *raison d'être*, however, have never even considered their responsibility to smaller neighborhood churches. Once the question of responsibility to these other churches has been raised, the answers begin to appear, and exploratory talks with leaders of the other parishes can begin. The downtown church, because of its prestige and access to leadership and funds, often can strengthen the morale of a local church enough to make the difference between desperation and hope. Skilled help can be found, denominational councils can be swayed, municipal leadership can be reached, and social action can be engaged in from a position of strength. The downtown parish must avoid, of course, the danger of patronizing, and it must lean over backwards to avoid assuming prerogatives which belong to the smaller parish.

CULTURAL CENTER FOR CHRISTIAN ART

In every inner city there dwell men and women with cultural interests and skills. The younger and more radical of these have been offended by the banality of the intellectual and artistic life the Church has shown them over the years. These are exciting, unusual, thinking people who, if Christians, usually do not feel at home in the family-centered organizational life of the suburban church. The downtown parish can be a lively part of their lives, if they are given an opportunity for the expression of their faith in their own terms within its walls. Jane Jacobs in her book, *The Death and Life of American Cities* (1961), points out that people come downtown nowadays for specialties they cannot

buy in the suburban chain stores which cannot afford to special-
ize. One comes downtown for diamonds and furs and Chinese
tea, not for underwear or hamburgers.

The downtown parish is subject to the same sociological forces,
and therefore must offer something *different* from what is offered in suburbia—art shows, professional-level chancel drama,
special music, seminars in Christianity and the arts, ballet with
Christian themes. Such functions fulfill the demand that the
Church be involved in the intellectual life of the city, provide
a useful evangelistic entrée to spectator and actor, and mean
that a Church home is available to people who often are in
desperate need of community and pastoral help. Art and music
are important to the worship of the Church; Psalm 150 indicates
this. The Judson Memorial Church in Greenwich Village, New
York City, is the outstanding example of this ministry.

A COUNSELING CENTER

To the doors of the downtown church come an incredible
variety of people with an incredible variety of problems. One
summer day in Indianapolis a man came for help; he was unable
to work because he had been mauled by a polar bear! Not only
are there the transients, but also men, women, and young people
who find themselves in the welcome anonymity of *downtown*
for many reasons: they may be dealing with broken marriages,
business failures, or mixed marriages not at home anywhere
else; they may be widowers, orphans, alcoholics, homosexuals,
government workers, people on temporary jobs away from home,
servicemen, and so forth. The downtown parish *must* be able to
deal with such persons either directly or by referral. We simply
cannot say, "We are sorry, we can't help you." Whatever special
vocation a downtown parish may have, the vocation of loving

concern for the individual in trouble must never be ignored. This means that no matter how skillfully other agencies are used, the clergy staff of a downtown parish must be larger in proportion to membership than that of a parish in a more stable neighborhood. It also means that the office workers, especially the receptionist who first sees such persons, must be trained to be warm and charitable, skillful in encouraging the timid and discouraging the bold. A valid lay ministry can be built up around the receptionist's desk of a downtown parish.

A COMMUNITY

For this type of church the development of a sense of community is the hardest task—and the most important. For some of those who come are in desperate need of human companionship. In a small parish a sense of warmth sometimes develops automatically; in a downtown parish its development must be fostered. The welcoming committee and the coffee hours, no matter how boring, are essential. But most important of all is the skillful transplanting of new persons into small groups where they will feel at home. Hence the need for a great variety of small group life within a large downtown parish.

It must be remembered, however, that some persons do not wish to do more than come to church on Sunday morning and that they have a right to this choice. For a multitude of good reasons they may need time to lick their wounds, to express their Christian vocation on their jobs or in family or neighborly tasks. For this reason one must strike a balance between warm invitation and overhearty regimentation. There should be at least one door through which people can leave the church undetected. As Paul Musselman was fond of saying, "Don't plug every door with a curate."

ANSWERING SPECIFIC NEEDS

SOCIAL ACTION

A witness in social action is an important ministry of the downtown church. The location in the central city gives it a special responsibility to be in touch with the city's social issues. A denominational Social Relations Department hardly takes the place of this aspect of the downtown ministry. Such a department is concerned with all issues which affect the life of the diocese, district, or presbytery; it must include refugees, service to the military, state and national legislation, and so forth. The downtown church must be concerned with the *city itself*.

It is downtown that things happen and that decisions are made, and usually the downtown church has within its congregation men and women who are in touch with almost every aspect of the city's life. Furthermore, in distinction from the neighborhood parish which may have as its parishioners only the lower economic groups, the downtown parish ordinarily has some of the so-called power structure within its membership. How this location and talent can be usefully harnessed to the demands of the gospel is a difficult question.

I cannot overemphasize the need for an active social action program in the downtown church. Such a program may alienate some people, but it will also draw people—not only the dispossessed who may benefit from such a program, but also alert churchmen who are looking for a parish which demonstrates its relevance to their lives as citizens and which is in touch with "what is going on." Such persons come *because* it is a downtown church; they do not come for sentimental reasons, *despite* the fact it is a downtown church. The downtown specialized ministry will draw over the years more and more of that kind of person and will build the leadership strength for future generations.

If social action and cross-section membership are avoided for fear of alienating the Old Guard, there will be no growing edge to replace them, and the church will grow old and suddenly die with a collapse frightening in its rapidity.

EVANGELISM

This brings us to that catchall word "evangelism." The author is among the clergy who are not ashamed to say that they care about numbers. Surely there are more important criteria for success, but numbers are people. The metropolitan downtown church, like Trinity on Wall Street, may have to rely on a weekday ministry and specialized functions to have a reason for being. But even there, in that most absurd of Sunday morning locations, an active congregation still worships. For all the adventuresome doings during the week, one must never neglect Sunday morning; one must make it as exciting and magnetic as possible and frankly worry when the attendance goes down.

All we have discussed has evangelistic overtones; the total life of the Church either draws or repels people from our Lord. It is also true that a drop in attendance must be measured against the whole program. At the same time, there should be present, if possible, in every congregation, a group whose sole responsibility is *new people:* how to get them, how to keep them, how to work them into a place where they can grow. Such a group would be the tie between a good Sunday morning "program" and the ongoing life of the parish family. To them would go all newcomers' cards. From them would come program suggestions to fill vacuums of needed organizations. Evangelism is usually not a one-to-one process, but rather a pulling of persons into the family life in one way or another. A rather sizable literature has grown up around the subject of lay evangelism. It seems to have been found necessary that such groups have some kind of prayer life together and a sense of being more than a committee, which indeed they are. The pattern for such may be found in *An Adventure in Discipleship* by Roger Lloyd.

The pattern in evangelism in many churches is of the "bring a friend" type. This is a good thing and should be encouraged by constant reminders. The device of having a "Visitors' Sunday" is a bit gimmicky, but nonetheless valid. This involves much hoop-la, letters, newspaper publicity if possible, and then a Sunday morning with emphasis on the visitor. There are explanations of the Episcopal Church, of the life of the parish, and extra-special coffee hours. Sermons on evangelism must recur; people easily forget their constant apostolic obligation. *But,* if the "bring a friend" program goes well, it often increases the monochromatic nature of the parish family, and the planning committee or minister should be conscious of lopsided gains in one or another social group. If so, special effort of a more unusual sort should be attempted.

The obvious example has to do with minority groups. The timing of evangelism in their direction is, of course, delicate, as is the manner of it. But as we all know, opening the doors is not enough to welcome people, and if there are no Negroes in the congregation, the "bring a friend" system will not increase their number. The same is true of the "working man" as over against the white-collar man. The dangers involved, in a mobile society, are stated very well by Gibson Winter:

. . . association by level of achievement is the dominant principle of informal relations. This means that the antennae of the congregation are extended into the community, picking up the wavelengths of those who will fit into the social and economic level of the congregation; the mission of the church is actually informal co-optation; the lay ministry is a means to recruit like-minded people who will strengthen the social class nucleus of the congregation. Churches can be strengthened by this process of co-optation so long as the environs of the Church provide a sufficient pool of people who can fit the pattern of economic integration; once the pool of recruits diminishes, the congregation is helpless—friendly contacts can no longer keep it going.[1]

This was written to the problem of the Church in a transitional neighborhood or in suburbia, but it can be an even more devastating process in the downtown church which can become the refuge of a like-minded group which, by its presence, turns away people from other groups. Since it takes an extra effort to bring people downtown in the first place, what would be a minor irritant in a neighborhood church becomes enough to keep people away from the downtown situation.

This viewpoint is open to criticism from the purists who say that people should always go to their nearest church. Although some of the values behind parish neighborhoods, such as a responsibility for *all* the people in a given area, are good, the principle becomes ridiculous in the United States where there are churches within a block of each other downtown. I emphatically favor the participation of suburbanites in the life of the downtown church. To overcome the artificialities of economic segregation ("The Suburban Captivity") we must foster other artificialities. The automobile caused suburban development; the autombile can also be the means of having people meet across the lines of economic standing in at least one type of parish. This brings us to a further point. A "bourgeois" membership can alienate the more humble members of the city; this danger must be met by such methods as establishing a neighborhood house in a low-income area or by overt doorbell ringing and "house church" work in areas where the denomination is not represented.

But the opposite dangers, although not so obvious in their appearance, are equally grave for *the downtown church*. If it

[1] Gibson Winter, *The Suburban Captivity of the Church* (Garden City: Doubleday, 1961), p. 72.

becomes a "lower middle-class" establishment, it will be almost impossible to lure the "upper middle-class" group into membership. To this some may say, "So what." Nonetheless, these people are needed for more than financing. They are also needed for their special contribution in terms of social action on the power-structure level, in terms of the weekday ministry to downtown, in terms of their being exposed to the problems of the inner city when they make their voice heard on the denominational council or on the boards of the various charitable institutions on which they serve.

The evangelism of the suburbanite to downtown is a subtle thing and must be handled most delicately. The minister himself, through personal contact, probably can do the most, but if there are wide-awake laymen on the lookout for men who have a growing edge of interest they can set up the necessary lunch. There is nothing more gratifying, for example, than seeing a typical suburban, bored Episcopalian become "fired up" in a downtown church. Perhaps the day will come when suburban clergymen will advise the transfer to the downtown church of those within their parishes who seem to have a vocation to this ministry. The institution of dual membership so useful to Trinity, Wall Street, might well be utilized elsewhere. (Most of the vestry at this archetypal downtown church are members of suburban churches as well.)

Evangelism in a downtown church, then, is far more than setting up a calling committee. It rests upon the establishment of a magnetic Christian force in the center of the city alert to draw to itself men and women from every walk of life who are attracted to the excitement of its varied ministry.

SPECIAL SERVICES

The regular Sunday services must be lively and their effectiveness tested. One would think that a service with fine music and good preaching would attract more people in a downtown situation than would the typical family service. In many a small city, however, the Family Eucharist is growing every year, while the more typical formal service at eleven o'clock is not. In a few years, with more high-rise apartments in the area, the reverse may be true. There are no rules which apply categorically. Let us consider for a moment the special services which can be a most effective witness and a means of involvement in various aspects of the city's life. The Cathedral of St. John the Divine in New York has developed a tradition for such things as these: the graduation of a class of nurses, the matriculation of a high school, the celebration of the anniversary of the Fire Department, the memorial services which occur with so many organizations. This may seem a sentimentalization of some rather secular occasions; however, these services bear witness, if a bit superficially, to the fact that the Church *is* involved and God is concerned whenever men and women are attempting to work constructively to some end. (Even the "Grace" before public meals which many of us resent is a reminder of the comprehensiveness of his care.)

The structuring of such services is a fine art, combining the tact of the diplomat with the skills of a liturgiologist—usually the former is more important than the latter! One must please the Camp Fire Girls *and* submit to almighty God an offering theologically sound, in fairly good taste, and centered more on God than on the Camp Fire Girls. At the New York Cathedral it has been demonstrated that a service can be "personalized," interesting to non-Christians, comprehensible to any onlooker in terms of what it is trying to say, and still decent and orderly, grand and moving, worthy of the best in liturgical expression. Music is a most important part of such a construction; the minister often must be in the role of mediator between the "outlandish" demands of the participants and the rigidity of the organist.

A by-product of such services, when well done, is to attract to the Church persons who have never sensed before the numinous of liturgical or semiliturgical action, and to have them feel, inarticulately, the power of the Holy Spirit drawing them to the beauty of worship. Perhaps unconsciously, these people realize that the classic modes of worship best express the fullness of life and can best show forth the City of God dwelling in the multitudinous affairs of mankind. One could venture to say that this is true because all good paraliturgical functions are based upon the rhythm of the Eucharist—the rhythm of penance, the Word, offering, intercession, praise and thanksgiving. One of the best discussions of the role of paraliturgical functions in parish life, although expressed in the Roman Catholic idiom, is in Abbe Michonneau's *Revolution in a City Parish,* chapter two.

CHRISTIAN EDUCATION

As with evangelism, Christian education cannot be separated from the total life of the parish. Usually, the downtown church has a rather small Sunday School for the obvious reason that most families with children go to the neighborhood parish. Nonetheless, it is important that there be a Sunday School so that younger families *can* come downtown without sacrificing their children's education. The only unique quality there is parallel to the adult situation; there are children from many more backgrounds represented. It is perhaps easier, also, to find skilled teachers because of the relative smallness of the school and the fact that many single professional people are drawn to a downtown parish. Thus the downtown church can be an experimental center for Sunday Schools.

In the organizational life of young people, however, barriers rise up on every side. It is asking too much of parents to bring their children "down" several times during the week, unless the occasion is essential. If the children are in a highly professional boys' choir, for instance, the effort would seem justified. Otherwise, more than one midweek trip seems disproportionate when it is added to the hyperactive life of most middle-class American children. However, if a group of inner-city children are in attendance, the same program outlined hereafter for the parish in an inner-city neighborhood would be appropriate. For the few parents who are concerned, who see their neighbors' children engaged in a round of parish activity, and who feel their own children are missing something, there are several alternatives. One is for the minister to discuss seriously with them, family by family, the possibilities for more family prayer life; or he might select a few neighborhood meeting places for midweek gatherings—the "house church" medium for children. The children could also be encouraged to go to midweek functions at a nearby church. This latter suggestion tends to split allegiance and to make the children wish to go there on Sunday, but usually this can be overcome if the parents explain to the children why they feel the family should continue to be part of the old parish.

For clergy especially interested and skilled in this field, the downtown church offers a real opportunity for experimenting. It cannot be drawn into the activist youth program of the average parish, which is being criticized in some quarters as perhaps doing more harm than good to the children's image of what a church should be. There is no reason why the curriculum for young people could not reflect the same social concern expected of the adult program. There is every reason for the children to learn that the purpose of the congregation is not primarily social, in the narrow sense. This is not one more activity to range alongside of Scouts or dancing class, but is something which transcends and penetrates them all. The downtown church gives children a chance to know their counterparts from other neighborhoods. This may go against the grain in children, as it does in adults, but it is a wholesome opportunity for developing understanding.

The Christian education of the adult congregation can follow normal lines in its content and method. There are obstacles of timing which are becoming more difficult to meet as our cities become less safe for travel in "off-hours." For this reason and because well-publicized educational ventures often draw from outside the parish, the most useful kinds of downtown educational ventures are short series or one-shot sessions, rather than the long-term, once-a-week programming possible in neighborhoods. Even when the congregation cannot attend in great numbers, the fact of the presence of conferences on race relations, ecumenical themes, or the liturgy tends to have an educational effect. Also, within the intimate group life which is hopefully present, a great deal can be done educationally. One of the most effective arrangements, if small and low-pressure, is a weekly Holy Communion breakfast, followed by discussion which ends promptly at a given time. This is usually a men's affair but could also be set up for professional women. (In the United States, the sexes still traditionally separate socially during the day.)

SPIRITUAL HEALING

Downtown is the logical center for the ministry of spiritual healing. This is not the place to enter into the pro's and con's of this ministry, but to mention, in passing, its deep effectiveness and some of the dangers present within it. This is an emotionally charged field. On the one hand, a person may want no part of it because it refuses to settle nicely into the categories of regularity and reason. On the other hand, if he has lost a sense of excitement in the daily round, he may go all out for "healing" as being the "real thing" in a church where he feels the Spirit has been long stifled. There are also ecumenical complications. Liturgically oriented parishes are often the place where this ministry springs up, and yet the participants often insist on being inclusive. This raises the questions of open Communion and of the difficulty of bringing to bear the steadying effect of the whole sacramental balance of the Catholic faith which many feel is necessary for the normalcy of such groups. Perhaps the majority of those involved are not and never will be Anglicans, for example. Each parish must work out these problems—painfully, with the guidance of the Spirit, and in humble charity. All of us must continue to be open to this guidance and not always expect the Spirit to blow down regular channels. This is an important and essential ministry; it can be exciting and need not be an "odd-ball" affair. Some extraordinary souls are drawn to our Lord through it, and some extraordinary things happen because of it.

The life of one group I know which is interested in spiritual healing revolves around a monthly Holy Communion service, including the laying on of hands, followed by the regular meeting. Special intercessions are read—or merely laid on the altar if they are too many to read. This guild is run by lay people entirely. Calling on the sick, sending out cards, keeping up an intercession list, and planning an annual Healing Mission are among their responsibilities. This is *not* a parochial group, and it includes persons from other denominations. But the base of its operations is a downtown parish.

HELPING THE AGED

Of all the types of parishes within the city, the downtown parish has the greatest number of elderly people within it. As the younger generation moves to the suburbs, the older people stay on downtown for reasons of deep sentiment. Many of them, moreover, are persons who have raised their children and have returned to the convenience of downtown living. Finally, in a downtown parish older people are more likely to feel wanted than in the strictly family atmosphere of suburbia. In any case, they make up a large percentage of the average downtown church.

The so-called problems of the aged are so complex a part of modern life that the implications of the Church for this ministry defy treatment in a brief space. It seems, however, that there are some basic principles which need stating as far as our specialized subject is concerned. First, because their needs are so great and the Church cannot meet them all, we should concentrate on those areas where the Church can make a peculiar contribution.

A great deal of money and energy seems to be used up nowadays in the ministry to a very few older people. Thousands of dollars are poured into church homes for the aged, but those who receive the benefit of these homes are a tiny minority of persons who have the good fortune of qualifying for their ministrations financially and denominationally. If these same funds were spent in proper social action toward the establishment of nondenominational or secular facilities, the results would have a far broader base. Salaries for social workers (and they need not, in this instance, be highly trained) could be raised, whereby more older people in nursing homes, hospitals, and private homes would be visited and their needs attended to. With the proper leadership of this kind, volunteers could be involved to a much greater extent than presently; a ministry of prayer to the shut-ins could be carried on by laymen, and the whole outlook of older people who are shut-in could be changed. They could be relieved of the greatest and most desperate of their problems: purposelessness and loneliness. These older Christians have a tremendous vocation—the vocation of intercessory prayer, offering prayers for those who need them and offering their own loneliness and suffering as part of the redemptive suffering of the Body of Christ. If the Church could concentrate on this, rather than on the endless administrative and money-raising details of church homes, she would be giving them what she alone can give—a Christian vocation and a proper preparation for death, which lurks in dark fear for the lonely and desperate, but which shines like a goal for those who are already involved in the worship of the Communion of Saints.

Secondly, the parish itself must be so oriented that those who do attend can be an important part of its life. This is not easy; older people often wish to dominate and are set in their ways. Yet they have contributions to make, a mellow wisdom and a perspective which the young often lack. A parish needs these things. The programming based on these perspectives should attempt not so much to serve the elderly as to find ways in which they can serve their Lord. Such a program requires patience and charity on the part of old and young. The local church should not only be able to point to the fact that there are x number of Golden Age Clubs using its facilities, but also to the fact that older people are involved in other parish organizations. We spoke earlier of the economic segregation of the modern city; the age segregation is just as acute and perhaps even more harmful in hidden ways. No great civilization has endured without the presence of older people in its councils and the respect for older people in its mores. Discarding them to institutions or to the downtown section of town, however comfortable and independent they are and however, from pride, they insist upon their happiness, is not the answer. The Church must attempt to redress this segregation within its total life.

Thirdly, there should be an attempt to understand older people on a deep level, realizing that one cannot generalize about them any more than one can stereotype any group, but that they do approach life from a different perspective. As they grow even older, this special perspective becomes more pronounced. A small novel called *Memento Mori,* by Muriel Spark, deals well with this subject.

Our concern for the aged is a positive one. They are persons, not objects; they should have something to say about their destiny and the destiny of the church to which they belong. In our thinking about their needs, let us first supply what only the Church can supply before duplicating efforts better administered by the secular. (This is not a criticism of "Homes for the Aged," but a plea that this not be the major effort of the Church.)

QUIET DAYS AND RETREATS

In the activism of ministering in ways described above, the classic temptation for American Christians is to neglect the reflective life of prayer. We see our religion as incarnational and involved, but no active work can prosper or be guided properly without our being in constant touch with the life of prayer. This is obviously a daily thing; nonetheless, one must dramatize its importance by retreats and quiet days. These two spiritual exercises should not be confused. One is not a substitute for the other. The purpose of a retreat is to *go away* from one's daily life in order to gain a different orientation to the deepest levels of one's relationship to God. The quiet day is a pause for a moment *within one's daily life* to see its meaning in relationship to God. We need both. The retreat should be organized from the base of parishes, but it must be conducted away from them. The quiet day should be conducted within the parish. The retreat can have as its subject the probing of the depths; a quiet day takes the problems of daily life and exposes them to God. It is always discouraging that quiet days and retreats are so ill-attended, but the only way to build involvement in them is by having them and by being sure that they are mentioned from time to time in preaching. Their emphasis is to build the daily prayer life of the people and to throw them back on the discipline of daily prayer, weekly Holy Communion, and, if they so choose, periodic confession.

LOOKING AHEAD

THE LAY MINISTRY

The perfect parish would not be concerned with this subject as a separate heading, for the ministry of the laity would be taken for granted. But this is not Utopia, and we still tend to consider the laity a "problem." It is clear that their role is involved in all the aspects of the parish life already mentioned, as well as in many more. One thing is assuming more importance in the thinking of the Church and may become the cutting edge of the Church of the future. This is the serious theological training of the laity so that their principal ministry may be the frontier of the Kingdom. In other words, laymen should be given the necessary theological tools to deal with their daily work in Christian terms and to be involved as vocationally oriented Churchmen in politics, civic groups, and business associations.

Gibson Winter has written a masterful paper on this subject, entitled *The New Christendom in the Metropolis*. His argument is based on the fact that the Church of the future cannot be institutionally oriented, but must think of itself in terms of servant-hood to the world. The vocation of the Christian is to *serve*, not to *be saved*. In order to effect this point of view and in order that the Church be heard in the vastly complicated disciplines of modern life with which the clergy are not always equipped to deal, laymen must be trained. The structuring of this training has not been worked out; it will probably take forms quite different from the regurgitation of seminary lectures on the part of the clergy. In fact, the clergy should bear in mind that they themselves will be students as well as teachers and that this process will take the form of dialogue. Whether this happens in the local church or on a higher denominational level would vary from place to place. But the downtown parish is a logical center for this training of the laity for the principal vocation to which God has called them.

THE FUTURE OF THE DOWNTOWN CHURCH

The downtown parish hopefully will become the training center and communication point of the Church and the heart of the city. It will become less like the "parish" churches, and more the crossroads, if you will, of the City and the city.

In London, the old City of London churches have worked out completely nonparochial ministries. One is the center for "The Samaritans," a sort of "suicides anonymous." Another ministers to French and Swiss Protestants; one specializes in marriage counseling and another in music. One is a center for merchant seamen; various military groups meet at still another. Quite by spontaneous accident, these separate vocations have emerged and have given these architectural shrines of Christopher Wren and others a real *raison d'être*.

Unknown roads lie ahead under the guidance of the Spirit. The metropolis contains the key to the future of civilization; the working out of its problems will contain the solution of the problems of modern living. The downtown church is in a pivotal position. May she remain vital and alive to the great vocation to which she is called and not become discouraged by the confusion which often seems so overwhelming.

8. *The Vocation of the Parish:*
Neighborhood and Transitional Parishes

TURNING from the classic downtown parish to a very different situation, sometimes only a few blocks from the core of the city, one may find in a blighted area a parish of the type which used to be called a "slum" parish. Increasingly one also encounters the so-called "transitional" parish. Usually it is a bit further from the core in that gray area which once was suburban but now has almost been left behind to succumb to the more drab aspects of the encroaching inner city.

THE INNER-CITY NEIGHBORHOOD PARISH

Today the terms used for the parts of cities which have substandard housing, a high incidence of social problems, and ghettoized minority groups are words like "depressed" and "blighted." It is necessary to have such terms to describe the obstacles faced by those who live in these areas and the impetus for the Church to remain there. However, as we think through the Church's program, we realize that these words should be discarded. This place is *home* for those who live there; although sympathy may be in order, a patronizing attitude is not. There are many values in the so-called blighted areas which are superior to those of the uptown and suburban areas.

The focus of the downtown church is the whole city in all its varied life; this is the world which this particular Christian community is called upon to serve. The neighborhood parish, on the other hand, is called to serve the particular part of the city within which it finds itself. This is its *primary* vocation. (Secondarily, as in every church, an attempt should be made to relate to the employment of those who are part of the parish family. However, since men rarely work near their parish church, this effort is usually best attempted in extraparochial ways.) It is because of this localized vocation that the program of the neighborhood parish is so different in emphasis from that of the downtown parish.

For the sake of simplification, we will not consider at this point the problem of relating the "Old Guard" to the new neighborhood emphasis. Here we will be concerned with the way an inner-city neighborhood church reaches out to the unchurched people of its environs. The first problem the church faces is the initial breakthrough into the neighborhood and the development of the contacts made in this initial attempt.

Residents of blighted areas have very little formal education. They are, for the most part, economically insecure. Life contains a series of hazards whereby at any moment a job may be lost because of some slight change in the business cycle (this is the manpower pool of a free economy). A landlord may evict a family, a son may be picked up by the police, a husband may not show up at night with his pay check, or a baby may be bitten by a rat. No human being can live subject to these chances of life without some psychological insulation. This insulation may consist of what looks like a casual attitude toward life or a standoffishness toward middle-class "helpers," who often tend to manipulate rather than understand. There may seem to be an amoral approach to marriage and sex (divorce is often financially impossible), a lack of proper concern for one's children, and a tendency to be late to appointments and to be sloppy about church responsibilities. These are generalizations, but they are true enough to affect the Church's approach.

There are stereotypes about the Church in the minds of inner-city people which make it doubly hard to reach them. White clergy or anyone white, in their minds, have some ax to grind. They cannot *really* care. Colored preachers, they say, are bossy and dictatorial and often are in the business for financial reasons. The Church, like anything else, is a racket and belongs to the old folks, or else it is a means of status advancement. Those who go to an integrated church or other than a storefront church are putting on airs.

On the other hand, on the positive side, there is wonder in the warmth and generosity which involuntary poverty gives to many people. Perhaps this is because there is so little to lose; one may as well share it. But one never ceases to be amazed at the welcome offered by Puerto Rican families to remote cousins or friends from the islands or by Negro families to others recently arrived from the South; at the willingness to care for nephews and nieces when there is not enough even for one's own; and at the way in which already overcrowded families will take in new groups to live with them. Another very positive trait is that once the Church has been accepted and the family has become a part of its life, the Church assumes a far more important role than with the "average" member; it becomes the center not only of worship, but of social life and social action, and the place to come when one has a problem of *any* kind.

A beginning must often be made with an old church building, almost deserted and locked during the week, and with a reputation for being segregated, unfriendly, and completely unrelated to the neighborhood. The best methods of destroying this image are working with children and engaging in social action. Both attempt to show the loving concern of the Church for the daily lives of everyone. Each has its danger. It is hard to go beyond work with children, and the church may become a place known only as a glorified day nursery. It is also hard to take the step from social action to evangelistic involvement in the life of the Church. With each technique, however, one becomes involved in people's lives; one establishes relationship and communication, and from there, other ways of development present themselves.

WORK WITH CHILDREN

This has been a method used successfully by those associated with the Urban Mission Priests and others working from the same premises. It is an easy and simple approach. A clergyman or layman goes out and walks around the streets until he comes across some children. He asks them if they would be interested in going to the park, having a club, or learning to sing. If they say Yes (which they almost always do) he finds out where their families live, calls on the families, and receives their permission for the children to come. Johnny brings his friends, and the program has started.

Some problems arise along the way. First, Johnny may belong to another denomination. This should be ignored; the major purpose of the program is to fill a neighborhood need for recreation with adult supervision and relationship with the children. In most areas, as the program advances, there will be enough unchurched children to establish a Sunday School. But the church cannot attempt to break up a gang of children because they are of different faiths; one cannot, for instance, exclude the Roman Catholic or Jewish children. How much "religion" should be in the program? One should in no way apologize for the Church, and in each situation one can pour into the work as much "religion" as seems advisable. This may be done through short chapel services, vacation church school programs in the summer, or by less direct methods.

The primary fact that must be continually emphasized is that God loves each and every one. This is communicated not by word so much as by actions of love and concern. The adults again and again are reminded that whether the ball team is good or bad and whether Johnny completes his bookcase or not are relatively unimportant matters compared to their establishing a real relationship with him as a Christian. Once he feels that the church is a warm place and a good place he has learned the primary fact of Christianity: God is love. It is not easy to act this out, for often the children are hostile. Once the initial fear and novelty have worn off, some will begin to take advantage of the place; they will break things, steal, and become angry.

If the love and patience of the workers is deep enough they will bring the children through this phase to a point of deep love and respect. C. K. Myers, in his book *Light the Dark Streets*, deals in depth with a group of such youngsters. The movie, *The Quiet One*, spells out the same theme with a seriously disturbed younger child. The trouble is that most people do not have the patience to love through the difficult period and are shocked by the seeming ingratitude shown to them. Their pride is hurt. The point is, of course, that the child is testing them out. He has been hurt so many times and betrayed so frequently that he is not about to trust the thin ice of adult relationships without jumping up and down on it long enough to see if it is really strong.

These random remarks add up to this: If a parish goes into the business of working with inner-city children it must be prepared for a rocky road and it must be willing to be roughed up one way or another. What often happens is that a group delicately puts its toes in the water, arouses the hopes of the children, and then at the first splash withdraws to the safety of suburbia with some such excuse as this: "The children do not really want to be helped." The early stages of this kind of program in Jersey City are described in Ross Sanderson's book, *The Church Serves the Changing City.*

SUMMER PROGRAM

Before leaving the subject of work with children, the institution of the "Summer Program" should be mentioned. This is a device whereby the need of college and, especially, seminary students for summer field work has been utilized by the urban parishes to increase their summer staffs. Perhaps some general principles should be suggested. The first is to "start small." Supervising summer workers requires a great deal of time and a certain amount of "know-how," which in the beginning can be developed with two or three workers. It should not be taken for granted that seminarians know what to do. They may not even be able to teach Sunday School very well; thus, close supervision is necessary, but freedom and flexibility for individual skills and initiative must be provided. There should be reports at least weekly and frequent staff meetings—perhaps a long one weekly in which general problems can be discussed in depth and a short one at least every other day for handling mechanical problems. The good of the work must take priority over the training of the workers, but, at the same time, everything possible should be done to make the summer significant. Seminars with local experts in various fields and opportunities to discuss the theological implications of urban work, for example, can provide this significance.

There are almost always personality problems (not only conflicts, but summer romances, which seem to thrive in this setting). The seminarians should be shown that these are part of the everyday life of a clergyman and must be dealt with. However, an urban summer program should *not* delve into the psychiatric levels of a "clinical training" program; the work is too demanding to add this additional pressure. The purpose of the program and a rather clear schedule should be provided at the beginning. Some programs may require a whole week of orientation. But whether the program is run on a tightly scheduled nine-to-five basis like a day camp, or whether it is up to the workers to schedule the meetings and activities of whatever group they work with, there should be plenty of suggested activities and also room for change as the summer progresses. The financing can often be secured through such sources as suburban churches and civic clubs. Most places pay about $300 for six to eight weeks and provide room and/or board and something toward transportation. However, this should be looked upon as a scholarship and not paid unless the student needs it. Some summer work camps ask the students to pay for the privilege of working!

Follow-up on a summer program can be a "traumatic" experience. The summer staff leaves, and the minister wakes up to find two hundred children swirling around the doors of the church asking for something to do. School takes care of part of this problem, but one must provide at least a means for weekly contact with the children reached during the summer. They will not all come back by any means, but if nothing is done, the whole effort of the summer is lost in terms of building up the permanent structure of the parish.

If a parish intends to start a summer program for the first time, it would be advisable for the clergyman to spend a few days in a parish where one is going on; he should at least have an extended interview with others who have had experience in this kind of effort. The names of such parishes and clergy can easily be secured. The National Council of the Episcopal Church provides summer training programs.

SOCIAL ACTION

Social action is a vital part of the life of a neighborhood parish for reasons other than the actual good it accomplishes. First of all, if the neighborhood is integrated or Negro (and a large proportion of inner-city neighborhoods are Negro residential areas because Negroes are unable, by and large, to buy in the suburbs because of "gentlemen's agreements" or the difficulty of securing mortgages), the Negro community expects the Church to take the leadership in social action. The history of Negro advance since the time of slavery has centered around the Church and continues to do so. The advance of the role of the lawyer within the NAACP has not displaced the prestige of Martin Luther King in the South or of Adam Clayton Powell in New York. If some denominations are to be more than "white men's churches" they must step into this role in those areas where Negroes are seeking justice.

Social action spells out the fact that the Church cares and that it is important in the daily life of the community. Without it, a ministry in a blighted area is hypocrisy. A pastor may visit a family which is living four or five to a room without proper plumbing or heat and paying exorbitant rent; its children are undernourished and diseased. He cannot cheerfully say "Jesus loves you," pat the children on the head, and go whistling on his way back to the warm comfortable rectory without at least knowing that the Church as such is doing everything it can to alleviate these conditions. Nor can people living under such conditions be much attracted to a Church which is not fighting for their rights.

The East Harlem Protestant Parish and its offspring in Chicago and Cleveland have, it seems, used social action as the opening wedge into the life of the community. It has been the principal vehicle of evangelism in the early stages. Through contacts made in this way, the parish has proceeded to build its community. This has presented some problems of involvement in the life of the Church at the beginning of the ministry, as it always does. Men will join in the fight for material gain but will not see the necessity for the Christianity which lies behind it. The Episcopal Church, on the other hand, has started with the community; in other words, it has attempted to gather together a nucleus of Christians, of people who came to be associated with the parish. From their needs and with their help the social action struggle has begun. But whether the initial drive into the neighborhood is social action, the ministry to children, or some other approach to people where they are in their material needs, sooner or later any lively church in the inner city will become involved in trying to change conditions around it. This is a field where serious mistakes can be made most easily. For the moment, however, let us consider its evangelistic power.

Only deeply dedicated Christians can establish a Bible class or prayer group within some apartment house; people simply are not always interested. It is not hard, however, to bring people together for a meeting which has to do with the exorbitant rent being demanded by a landlord. If the establishment of such a group coincides with a current need (as, for instance, the lifting of rent controls in New Jersey in the early 1950's), the parish can become the center of a movement of vital concern and can begin to erase the image of unconcern which it probably has developed over the years. Furthermore, such groups are a way of reaching new people on their own level and of establishing relationships which may well move into the area of the pastoral and hence bring men to know our Lord.

The clergy must not be afraid to do the ridiculous and the improbable, to speak on street corners with an introductory interlude of "rock and roll," or to drive around town in a motorcade with play equipment on a truck to proclaim the need for playgrounds. The much publicized turning on of the lights illegally in the St. Timothy, New York, better housing campaign is a case in point. One must be sure (as sure as is humanly possible) that the cause is just and that one's facts are right. These battles, the preparation for them, and the excitement that surrounds them give an air of vitality which is contagious and makes it crystal clear that the Church is alive and on the side of "the people."

COMMUNITY

The need for community is just as necessary, if not more so, in the neighborhood parish as in the downtown church, but the form it takes is quite different. The parsonage or manse, if it is nearby, or the parish house kitchen becomes the "hearth" of the parish family. At all hours of the day and night, a coffeepot is on the stove and someone or other is "hanging around." This is a warm place out of the storm for children and for the lonely; it is a planning table for campaigns; it is the symbol around which men and women and children come to know each other and, hopefully, come to know the Lord. Every effective neighborhood parish has some such gathering place, differentiating the Church from the settlement house or social agency. It is the strength of the clergy as well as the drain on their energies.

Each "open rectory," as the Urban Mission Priests call it, has its own characteristics; some are more "open" than others, depending upon the needs of the rectory family. Some have coffee and sandwiches available once a day for anyone who needs them, and often the most desperate derelict can develop a friendship here which can bring him a step or two along the way to salvation. Some have children always playing in the yard—hopscotch, skiprope, kickball. Some have old ladies sitting in the shade of the stoop, passing the time of day. Some have combinations of these; it is a good thing for the children to learn charity toward the old men, and it is a good thing for the old ladies to find out that some of the children are "really quite sweet," as they would put it.

This community life is not always welcomed by next-door neighbors. Grace Church, Jersey City, was the subject of a petition not long after the new clergy came into residence. One night the rectory was the battle objective of a "rumble" between the white boys of the neighborhood and the parish's Negro boys. Often, noises of joy and anger would emanate from the yard and parish house. These may have made the parish a "bad neighbor," but it showed the world that the church was a twenty-four-hour institution of importance in the lives of many people.

PASTORAL WORK

In the downtown church, pastoral work tends to be formalized. People secure appointments to see the clergy, and the clergy call on them in the hospital. This is not so in the neighborhood parish. Calls in the hospital are frequent, but formal counseling sessions are very rare. Counseling is done on the stoop or over the eternal kitchen table; it is done as soon as the person who has a problem is able to reach the rectory; for the most part the problem is not one which can be put off. A child has been arrested; a husband is violent; or the landlord is evicting. The long-term relationships often growing out of such crises can follow a therapeutic direction; but usually this consists of five minutes here or there, an afternoon call if luck sets up a quiet time in the home, counseling, as it were, by the seat of one's pants. Clinical training which presupposes "the fifty-minute hour" cannot be transplanted bodily into a neighborhood situation.

The basic principles learned from clinical training are still true, even if they need to be expressed in a different idiom. Those who have lived a long time in the inner city have developed some useful ways of dealing with reality which are not in the textbooks, and until one comes to have the "feel" of this kind

of living it is rash to be directive, even though the course taken
by the counselee may make one's bourgeois hair stand on end.
Father Schlueter, a wise old priest who spent his life in an inner-
city parish (St. Luke's Chapel, New York City), once said the
poor cannot afford to be without luxuries. It is often more important for the over-all good of the family for the mother to have
a new Easter hat than for the children to eat supper. A new
shiny car for one deprived of a new shiny home may be a symbol
of self-respect absolutely essential for existence. We once took
a disturbed boy into the rectory to live, thinking that this would
be the best thing in the world for him. It was not. He became
much more disturbed; the pressure of our standards of behavior,
while seeming minimum for us, was too great for him. His
mother had resisted the idea; she was right!

The ministry in such an area is a rough and tumble life marked
by little structure and few rules. Those involved must rely completely upon the strength and guidance that comes from prayer
and the sacraments, upon love and patience—endless patience—
and the vigor and joy and laughter which is never far away from
the most tragic of situations.

ORGANIZATIONAL LIFE

If the parish plant is large enough, work with the children
relies heavily on recreation through which warm relationships
with them can be developed. Although there is a danger in the
parish's becoming just another settlement house and therefore
selling short the special gift of the Church, some kind of program
must be a base for the movement of love and grace. Baseball
teams, craft classes—even such an improbable but highly successful craft as jewelry-making for teen-age boys ("Look, I made
my old lady a jool!")—are all ways of becoming involved with
the young people of the area. Teen-agers take a tremendous
amount of time and involve great pressures on the parish and the

clergy if one goes beyond the churchy mamma's boys which can be found in any parish. It is wise, therefore, to start with children twelve and under. One of the real problems with teen-agers is working them into anything like the normal life of a parish. I will never forget one "gang" moving in to look over a ladies' bazaar, with scowling faces, hats turned down, and overcoats turned up. The flutter and screams were audible as the good ladies swept their precious wares under the tables. Yet a ministry to this teen-age group is essential and can be dealt with in some neighborhoods without too much strain. Elsewhere, in the very large cities, it is almost necessary to have a separate establishment or to work with this age group outside the parish, as the detached street workers of social agencies have come to do.

Whether the work be with teen-agers or with younger children, there is always the need for additional staff. The sooner some of the parents can be worked into this the better, but almost always there is a need for outsiders at the beginning. Here one must look "uptown" or out to the suburbs for leadership. This kind of relationship is not a new idea and, with proper care in selection and supervision, can be most effective. One should watch out for the lady bountifuls, those who like to "slum," but even those who may start with motivations of this kind can be taught, with the help of the Spirit, to come into the situation as equals, without sentimentality, and with a willingness for hard work. They will often find a new vocation here and even become members of the parish. We used to call them "fans," and without them we could not have existed in Jersey City. I remember the reservations I had about a very sophisticated actor taking on the direction of a play with a teen-age group. This turned out to be one of the best things that ever happened. We soon heard the kids using such phrases as "Dahling, you were wonderful!" By-products of this participation, of course, are public relations and financial help from outside the parish.

The adult organizational life of the neighborhood parish, like the pastoral work, is inclined to be rather less formal than in a conventional situation. Mothers' clubs are a natural beginning with a child-centered opening program. Men's clubs find more work than in most places because of the continual need for maintenance in old buildings. Social action projects pushed forward by *ad hoc* groups take up the energy of the more vigorous. Bible classes can be most effective if geared to the lives of the people. The House Church as described by Ernest Southcott in *The Parish Comes Alive* gives a structure to all sorts of patterns and brings to bear upon the parish life a missionary spirit, an outgoing apostolic movement valuable in its own right. Canon Southcott is fond of saying, "Pitchfork them out into the neighborhood!" The Eucharist, Bible classes, confirmation classes, social action cells, prayer groups—the variety is endless, and the importance of this variety is seen in reaching neighbors who never would come directly to the church. (Do we realize what a major step it is to gather oneself together, dress up, and come to a strange church?) Such activities make true missionaries out of those who accompany the clergy or conduct the groups themselves.

I recall one delightful Bible study group I had among some Puerto Rican families. I could read but could not speak or understand spoken Spanish, so we worked out this arrangement. I sat in a big chair with a Spanish-English dictionary on one arm, a Spanish Bible on one knee, an English Bible on the other knee, and a bilingual teen-age Spanish girl on the other arm of the chair. I would read in Spanish and ask a question in English. She would translate the question and the group would discuss it with great vitality. She would relay the main points, and the dialogue would continue. The age range was from a great-grandmother to a sleeping infant. We all had a marvelous time, and after a while most of the participants found their way to the parish church and the altar.

Flexibility, fluidity, imagination, and a willingness to set up meetings to which no one comes on time (or perhaps at all) and to patiently sustain "failure" are the keys to the "organizational" life of this kind of parish.

CHRISTIAN EDUCATION

As has been stated already, the main thrust of religious education in the parish is the *acting out of the love of God.* The children playing in the yard learn respect for the transient alcoholics. People of all ages become involved in social action protest demonstrations whose success is prayed for in the Eucharist. The parish learns from the fact that the clergy visit the hospital, the jail, and the police station; it comes to accept continually all people, from whatever background and with whatever reputation. The cheer and joy of the Christian fellowship is in itself religious education (one lady said that when she was too sad to smile she would come to the rectory because it was such a happy place); so too is the sheer beauty of the liturgical action ("When I first came to this church I thought I was in heaven," said an ex-fundamentalist). The total life of the parish is religious education.

A few comments can be made about education on a more formal level. First, teachers and facilities may be lacking and some kind of less-than-perfect compromise used. The clergy may have to take large groups into the church for formal instruction and story telling. The technique and approach of Father Wilson's *Haggerston Catechism* have proven to be helpful and effective in such a situation. (One may choose, of course, to alter the content.) Children can act out Bible stories as the clergyman does the narrating. Many easy and informal methods by which the subject matter can be fixed in the children's minds are available:

slides, flannel boards, blackboards. The parish does not *have* to have one room for each age level. The Sunday School certainly must not be limited because there are not enough classrooms; the church can be used. We have so many stereotypes about religious education; but there were no Sunday Schools at all until a hundred years ago, and the Church existed for eighteen hundred years or more without them.

Secondly, many of the curriculum materials are so full of suburban allusions and are graded so accurately for suburban children's achievement levels that they are almost useless. They are also quite expensive and presuppose fairly regular attendance and all the tricks of the trade including teachers who are at least high school graduates. There are some classic comments about curricula based on different ways of life. A lesson starts with the story of home life in which the opener is, "Mother came downstairs for breakfast." "What was she doing in someone else's apartment last night?" the city child asks. Another comment is: "God is your Father." The response may be: "Does he get drunk and beat me up?" These may be old chestnuts, but they point up the communication problems of the inner city.

However, it is heartening to know that several denominations are now preparing curricula specifically adapted to inner-city Christian education. Interdenominational committees are also working on such materials.

Tardiness is another problem which is especially prevalent in this work; therefore, the lessons should be not only fairly self-contained to take into account absenteeism, but also suitable to absorbing latecomers. There are some ways of dealing with lateness. If the children *enjoy* Sunday School they are likely to arrive earlier. Enjoy it they must for there will be little parental pressure in most cases. This puts an added burden on the teacher; the audience is not captive. Frankly, this can be a most useful discipline. A church bus, if the parish can afford it, helps promptness and attendance. A bus is almost a necessity in a parish where there may not be many cars available for rides when it is necessary to take a group somewhere. A parish may begin with neighborhood people; but then these people move, and until the denomination has friendly churches all over town, they may wish to come back to their old parish. If it is a small city or if they have not moved too far, a bus can be used to pick them up. A bus also saves a good deal of money in the summer program.

The greatest problem in education is lack of reading ability and the great variety of skill among children of the same age group. This problem can be met with imagination by the use of stories which appeal to all ages, by individual attention to those who are way behind or far ahead, and by supplementary activity as the program goes along. Above all, it must be remembered that even in the Sunday School it is more important for the children to love and feel loved by the teacher than for them to know the dates of the Exile. A surly sexton can cancel out years of classroom teaching on the love of God.

FINANCE

The business of finance is always uppermost in the minds of church leaders when work in the inner city is mentioned. When asked, "Are you doing anything?" they usually reply, "We do not have the money." If this is the only reason why nothing is being done, it is difficult to see why things are being done in some dioceses, districts, and presbyteries and not in others. The answer is that some of these groups care enough to make money available and others don't; some give the work high priority and others do not.

There is money available, but it is often being used for other more "rewarding" ministries—financially rewarding. It is often being used for ministeries where "success" is more clearly dis-

cernible. Sometimes it is being used to bring more congenial
people into the Church rather than to bring in people from
different backgrounds who one day may embarrass the Church
by inordinate demands and radical views.

The problem of finance is not simply that. It is a problem of
conversion to the work both on the higher level and within
the inner-city parish itself. Again there are some principles worth
stating.

The best way to raise money is by starting a program and asking support for it afterwards. By hook or crook the parish should
get a few thousand dollars to get the program off the ground;
then there will be more than an idea to publicize. Once a program, however small, is begun, pictures can be taken, visits can be
made, speakers can barnstorm, foundations can be approached,
suburban and uptown parishes or groups within them can be
asked to adopt part of the program, brochures can be mailed to
all and sundry (urban work is most photogenic), and the neighborhood can be involved in money-raising projects.

Within the parish, the pledge system should be maintained
and supplemented with proper stewardship education, but it
cannot be relied upon as heavily as in most conventional parishes.
The people just don't operate that way. Instead, there have to
be different "affairs": dances, bus rides, pew rallies (everyone
buys a pew for a special service), and boat rides. Charts in the
back of the church and other visual aids are useful. One has to
tread the line between the traditional money-raising customs of
indigenous churches, which sometimes are too competitive to be
allowable, and the fact that the staid "every member canvass"
approach does not work. One could learn from watching a skillful minister of a fundamentalist sect draw money from the congregation. It may take him two hours, but he raises amazing
sums. "Who is going to give twenty dollars? Do I hear twenty
dollars? Come now, I need ten gifts of twenty dollars! Yes, there
at the back? Mrs. Jones? Come on down to the front, Mrs. Jones.

Give her a hand now, folks; Mrs. Jones has given twenty dollars. How about fifteen dollars?" To most of us this is embarrassing, but to some congregations it is part of the fun. Not many conservative clergy could or would use this method, but imagination is necessary to raise money among people who may be accustomed to this method.

Outside the parish, the diocese, district, or presbytery must be lobbied continually. Beyond obtaining a share of its budget and the benefit of special drives, it is often possible to establish adoption programs with more stable parishes. This has its perils of dependency, but it can be done well.

Money raising of any kind can be facilitated by cooperative ventures which have more appeal than does the support of a single parish. The cooperation could be a joint inner-city venture or a "pie slice" or "sector" cooperation, whereby suburban churches are part of a subdivision within which some inner-city congregations lie.

This has been an arbitrary review of the program of the inner city and needs to be supplemented by further reading on the subject. Listed in the Bibliography under *The Urban Church at Work* are books which provide a gold mine of ideas and anecdotes drawn from Los Angeles and Marseilles and Johannesburg. One final comment is in order: the inner city can never settle down to a routine, no matter how effective that routine may be. As one of our former parishioners once said, people in the inner city want Bread and circuses. In concentrating on the Bread we can't forget the circuses; as the Bread symbolizes the life of the Christian, the circuses show the liveliness of the Church.

THE TRANSITIONAL PARISH

Modern metropolitan areas have a core, a blighted area usually surrounding the core, and suburbs. Each kind of place suggests certain ministries and responds to certain ministries. However, there is another kind of place, which is increasing in number with the metropolitan "sprawl"—the gray, transitional areas which were built to be suburbs but are rapidly taking on the qualities of life of the inner city. They are characterized by a relatively low density of population and a corresponding lack of vitality, a drabness and monotony which even the worst sections of the blighted areas of high density do not have, and an insecurity in their institutional life. The older residents move out and weaken the institutions they have built up over the years, and the newer residents have not had the chance to build their own institutions which fit their special needs.

This is the area of the one-family house converted to the rooming house; it is the area of racial tension, as block after block is "busted" and former white residents feel it necessary to move. In these houses the residents consist of elderly people who out of sentiment, stubbornness, or lack of funds do not leave or of younger people who have not "made the grade." Into the area come single people, transient rooming house residents who will never feel at home in the community, nursing homes which benefit from the low real estate values, and members of minority groups who find such a place the only exit from life deep in the ghetto or perhaps literally the only place they can find to live at all.

The suburbs have their well-oiled institutions: churches, neighborhood committees, PTA's. The long-term "slums" have theirs: churches, settlement houses, NAACP's, ethnic associations of one kind or another. The gray areas, however, have none of these and, as is obvious from the description, the material from which one would build an institutional life is not very promising in its leadership content or its loyalty to the neighborhood. The Church usually finds herself involved with the old neighborhood pattern. She is one of the institutions which have been there for some time and quite obviously are part of the past.

This is the dilemma. Theoretically, the Church in such an area should be welcoming the newcomers and endeavoring to assist them in building the new community life and facing the future. However, the newcomers are the *very* thing which the old-timers fear. In fact, they symbolize not only the defeat of the neighborhood (from the old residents' point of view) but the defeat of life itself. Christians are taught to turn to their Lord in time of trouble. They automatically turn to the Church in time of need; but instead of openly seeking help from Christ on his terms, these Christians may seek to make the church an oasis of the "good old days." The more members who leave or die, the more defensive and less evangelistic the remainder become. Congregational life tends to become neurotic, and it is almost impossible to deal with it, no matter how many good ideas are available.

Some feel that such a place has to die before it can be rejuvenated. This is possible when the finances are limited; but if there is enough endowment to continue, the parish may drag on for generations. The bishop attempted to close one such church in an eastern city thirty years ago. It is still open. The only answer is one of realism. Someone should patiently but firmly try to bring the parish around to more enlightened thinking; this can sometimes be done. If this proves impossible, perhaps the denominational officials must be rather cold-blooded and let the parish die or receive help only with the provision that a forward-looking program be instigated. There is no blueprint for this kind of thing; it is a human problem. The obstructionists cannot be treated as things; they are people with very real problems. On the other hand, it does them no good to be allowed to live in a dream world surrounded by unrecognized fears. The purpose of an enlightened ministry in such a parish would be to show the old-timers, who have ceased to have much of an objective in life, that they have a great contribution to make to the new neighbors. This is happening in many places. A new program is started along the lines previously mentioned; there is a big parish row; some die-hards leave, but others remain and catch the vision.

The program takes on a three-fold aspect. First, there is the old organizational life. Sometimes, especially with older people, it is wise to allow this to go along pretty much "the way it used to be." Such small groups give the members a reason for being; they may be too old to change, and they can continue with their sewing or card parties relatively undisturbed. Secondly, there are the established groups where there is some possibility of bringing in new people. A rather "polite" ladies guild may well be the kind of thing older middle-class Negro women enjoy, and it can take on new life within its limited range when these "newcomers" become a part of it. Thirdly, there will be such new structures as have been described, based on the new break-through into the neighborhood. Naturally, there will be conflict between these groups, and a great deal of patient interpretation will be necessary on both sides, but it is possible, though difficult, to work this through. Over the years a gradual change in emphasis can come about in which the new groupings assume more and more importance.

The person who gets caught in the middle is the clergyman. He must be emotionally stable in order to endure the pressures and the failures. He must try not to be caught up in hostility toward the old-timers. He must rely heavily upon our Lord and see himself as doing an exciting piece of work which has to pass through this difficult stage. Above all, he must have a community of support with other clergy who are in the same predicament. The bishop or ecclesiastical authorities must stand firmly behind him, encouraging him and putting him in touch with sources of inspiration and new ideas.

The basic problem, of course, is that such parishes should have begun to change long before the feeling of defeatism touched them. Foresight in their leadership can begin to change the face of the parish while there are still leaders within it. This would be relatively simple. However, the human reaction is to ignore the signs and wait until very late in the game to face the fact of change.

One useful technique in dealing with a changing neighborhood is to help the congregation become educated concerning the movements going on around it. Knowledge casts out fear, and often the worst fears are not justified. Even though the truth is rather strong meat, if the parishioners know the facts and are given constructive jobs to do—either in arresting the change or dealing with it—this very action tends to dissipate fear and to bring persons into an involvement with the forces which swirl around them. It gives them a feeling of strength, whereby they no longer are mere objects being tossed about by sociological change, but now are part of the process; they can *do something about it*. The problem here is to avoid this energy's being diverted into merely a blocking process against newcomers. If the parish takes the leadership in establishing, for instance, a cleanup campaign or in forming a citizens committee to enforce zoning regulations, a dead and fearful neighborhood can become a place of hope. The techniques of such organizing can be learned. The discipline of community organization has quite a literature, and any large city will have persons trained in these techniques who would be glad to assist in such a program. If one starts asking at the Health and Welfare Council or its equivalent he will soon track down someone who can help. Usually there will be some vestigial groups already in existence in the neighborhood who only need fresh leadership to function again.

Within the parish itself, or in conjunction with nearby churches of other denominations who face the same problems, one can set up many opportunities for meeting the new neighbors and for educating the old-timers in the area of race relations and human relations of all kinds. Again, the disposition of superstition and stereotypes will do much to allay fears.

Whatever the pattern of the parish's life, the clergyman and whatever enlightened leadership remains (usually there are three or four stalwart laymen who, by the Grace of God, are still there and who will become excited by new life) should rather clearly define the purpose of the parish and the priority of the program. Honest self-study is in order. We must be really willing to take the plunge into neighborhood evangelism; we must not undertake it to salve our own consciences when secretly we would like things to stay as they used to be. We must care about the welfare and conversion of the old-timers and not really want to get rid of them.

The parish has to pinpoint its effort toward one clear goal at a time, so that its image to the changing neighborhood is vivid. Once a goal or a special vocation is established, realistic plans can be made—and they must be realistic. If they are too ambitious, they will bring more sense of failure; if they are not idealistic enough they will not inspire the parish. Finally, the criteria which must be always before the parish are service and involvement. There is perhaps a greater field for service for the small parish in a changing neighborhood than anywhere else in the city. The Church is the reconciler par excellence, and people who trust each other as Christians can begin to overcome other hostilities. In addition, the Church can be the place where people can deal with what seems like defeat, can find warmth in a world which grows continually cold, and can find meaning in the most confusing of situations.

THE SUBURBAN PARISH

Any lengthy discussion of the suburban ministry would be out of order here and beyond the competence of the author. However, this much should be said: the suburban parish must realize that it is not isolated from the inner city; the money that keeps it going comes from the commerce and industry whose workers live in the inner city or depend upon the inner city indirectly. Further, it must realize that those who live downtown are neighbors; the gospel says nothing about propinquity as a definition of neighbor. Finally, it must be aware that the inner city is a missionary opportunity. The problem of the suburban parish as it faces the city is "out of sight, out of mind." There must be increasing dialogue among the diversely located parishes in the cities so that they all can feel that they are *the Church in the city* and not separate, lonely institutions whose thriving or dying depends upon their luck in location. We are all the Body of Christ, and this Body cannot be divided.

9. Urban Work and the Diocese, District, or Presbytery

"There is, it seems, a law in things that if a man is compelled to choose between two good actions, mutually exclusive, the one which he chooses to neglect will in course of time avenge itself on him."

—CHARLES WILLIAMS

THE modern city is so complex, mobile, and interrelated that an approach to its ministry must be coordinated at least on the level of the diocese, district, or presbytery. There are those who feel that in view of the so-called "strip cities" which include many municipalities in a contiguous "sprawl," the Church should coordinate her work on what may turn out to be a provincial or regional level.

The responsibility of the higher echelon of diocese, district, or presbytery is demonstrated in the Episcopal Church at the consecration of a bishop when he receives a copy of the Holy Scriptures and is given this charge: "Hold up the weak, heal the sick, bind up the broken, bring again the outcasts, seek the lost." Thus the responsibility for the people of the cities rests squarely upon the diocese. The complexity of discharging this responsibility can only be properly understood after recognizing the causes of the problems.

SOME CAUSES OF THE "URBAN CHURCH PROBLEM"

1. *Mobile Population.* The primary external cause of the Church's weakness in certain areas of the city is the mobile population. I think of a particular parish in New York City, past whose doors have come seven waves of immigration: Irish, German, Italian, Polish, Jewish of all nationalities, Southern Negro, and Puerto Rican. Each wave has left in its wake its weak members, while the strong, in their second generation, have gone forth from the slum to more inviting shores. Every urban parish has been exposed to at least one such movement. Maintaining a strong parish structure through such changes requires an unusually creative sense of vocation.

2. *Inadequate Parochial Philosophy.* The parish, by and large, has thought of itself as a group of spiritually like-minded people who receive the ministrations of the Church, those who "attend the Methodist (or Episcopal or Congregational) Church." The diocese has, for the most part, acquiesced to this philosophy, with occasional encouragement to reactivate the lapsed or to involve other like-minded souls in the ordered round of parish life. Such inadequacies not only weaken and make irresponsible the work of the particular parish, but also tend to encourage parochialism and a lack of responsibility of one parish for another.

3. *Lack of Cooperation.* Take a particular metropolitan area like Indianapolis. It is a small enough city to analyze fairly easily. We have one strong downtown parish (the Cathedral) and two weak urban neighborhood parishes (one of which is predominately Negro), no one of which has been ministering to its

neighborhood until recently; two strong suburban parishes; and about five new suburban parishes or missions on the fringe of the city in various stages of rather rapid growth. Unless there is cooperation, the two small inner-city parishes will die. The cooperation which has been lacking has been in terms of leadership and financial assistance.

4. *Lack of Leadership.* The most deeply discouraging factor in inner-city church life is the absence of leadership ability or leadership drive. The people who remain are often frightened, beaten, defensive people. If anyone attempts to lead them, he soon becomes discouraged. The more these people fail, the more exclusive and defensive they become. Furthermore, the real leaders have, for the most part, probably left the blighted area long ago. To compound the weakness, old or broken clergymen have often inherited these situations.

5. *No Realization of the Missionary Character of Urban Work.* A few years ago there was established by the French Roman Catholic Church a new missionary enterprise called "The Mission to France." The French leadership realized that France was a pagan country. Think for a moment about this. Is it true, to some extent, of the United States, especially in the inner city? And if it is true, one must realize the *radical* changes in thinking this recognition necessitates. It means, among other things, that a mission is a place from which the gospel is sent to a pagan culture. This entails a deep problem of communication and an infusion of leadership and funds from the outside.

6. *Lack of Financial Assistance.* The financial councils of any enterprise wish a rapid return on the dollar, but such a return is not always the most important factor in the ultimate success of the enterprise. In the church, the new mission in the cellophane suburb is a glittering investment and often yields a rather rapid return. However, if financial assistance in the city is not rendered

and the Church becomes merely a suburban institution, the Church will lose its soul and its very life. The urban mission to the inner city is essential to the life of the Church; and financial aid is essential to this urban mission.

7. *Absence of Long-Range and Courageous Planning.* Each one of us can think of cases where the closing of one parish which a careful sociological study indicates to be without a future and the intensive support of another parish in a key neighborhood would have been far better than the back-breaking and purse-draining procedure of pouring too little down the drain in both parishes.

URBAN CHURCH PLANNING

In planning for a military campaign of any kind you first decide (or usually the higher echelon decides for you) what your mission is. You then proceed to work out the fulfilling of the mission and finally combine it in the classic operation order, something like this: (1) information about the terrain and the enemy; (2) information about our own troops; (3) mission of the operation—over-all and individual; (4) supply; and (5) communication.

Let us use this scheme in working out a framework for planning at a departmental level in the diocese, district, or presbytery.

The *terrain* has to do, in our case, with the sociological factors present and projected in a given city. The diocese must be continually seeking data on which to base its planning. What is the age-profile of a given area? A military unit does not use tanks in a jungle campaign; we do not need a basketball court in a high-rise apartment area mostly inhabited by retired people. It is most important that such research be done at a church district or Church Federation level. The entire metropolitan area must be investigated, since each part is dependent upon the other.

Several books have been written about church district planning, and a great deal of such material is available in other forms.

A new field of study has been developed as clergy of various churches have sought to relate sociological facts to the life of the church. Among those doing outstanding work in this area are the Rev. Joseph Moore of the Episcopal Church, the Rev. Merrill Ruoss, until recently in charge of the Urban Division of the National Council of Churches, and the Rev. Gibson Winter. The best available book on the subject is *Urban Church Planning*, by Walter Kloetzli and Arthur Hillman. Material on this subject is also contained in *The Effective City Church*, by Murray H. Leiffer. These books also consider such topics as self-study plans for urban parishes and sources of sociological information in the secular community, the use of census tracts, and the determination of which industrial units will have population movements projected. There is a wealth of information already available in every community and also, certainly in any large metropolitan area, competent lay persons who can be called upon to interpret such information for the Church. In the Diocese of Indianapolis, for instance, a business sociologist from Indiana University took a leave of absence to staff the Episcopal Diocesan Planning and Strategy Commission. The important point is this: no one parish has the resources to search out the necessary data for its own planning. Research in each city should be done at a higher level within the denomination or, preferably, at the level of the Church Federation or Council of Churches. No modern industry dares to operate without a knowledge of the "market" and its movement; huge sums are allocated to research divisions. Yet the Church often fails to spend that first dollar to wisely plan her investments and growth.

INFORMATION ABOUT THE ENEMY

If there are no theological objections, let us call our adversary the Devil, "who goeth about seeking whom he may devour." In the causes of failure and through research some of the Devil's strength and the way he has deployed his forces become apparent. He has been rather successful; let us hope he is complacent. A rather careful reconnaissance may be indicated to feel out the strength of his position. For instance, there may be a certain parish which is about to be closed down. There is a nagging sense of guilt about its closing. What is recommended? There should be reconnaissance in force—an intensive three- or four-year program of a vigorous neighborhood ministry of witness, service, and evangelism; a witness of sharing the life of the people who *live* around the parish; a ministry of love to the needs of the neighborhood whatever they may be; and a teaching of the faith to those who are attracted to the warmth (and may it truly be warm) of such a community. If such a program is unsuccessful in terms of response and fulfilling of the Church's basic mission, the parish should be closed; the enemy's forces are too strong. If, on the other hand, there is human response to the ministry of love, whether it take the form of Golden Age clubs, pastoral counseling, youth recreation, or street-corner preaching, the ministry should be continued and, if possible, intensified. The parish made a breakthrough.

INFORMATION ABOUT FRIENDLY TROOPS

This would include, to continue the analogy, knowledge of the program and plans of other churches. Whatever one's feelings about interchurch cooperation, it is important to know what is afoot. In some extreme cases, as in the Cleveland version of the East Harlem Protestant churches, the Episcopal Church is working in organizational unity with an interdenominational parish (a group of chapels sharing staff and resources), while safe-guarding her theological position and sacramental integrity within her own chapel life. In other places, there is careful planning not to overlap activities, but to complement the social service offered by each parish. An interchurch venture is beginning in Indianapolis, whereby a group of neighborhood churches, each backed by the diocese, district, or presbytery, respectively, are launching a jointly financed "crash program" in a twenty-block inner-city area. (This program is described in greater detail elsewhere as a type of ecumenical approach.) One could ring the changes on this kind of cooperation, but the main thing is not to injure each other's efforts. There is plenty of work for all, and any kind of unfriendly competition will injure the image of the Church in the city just as surely as it has been so injured in the foreign mission field. On the other hand, the services which are claimed may not actually be going on and meeting the needs of the people. The mere fact that a church has a large gymnasium in a slum neighborhood does not necessarily mean it is touching the delinquency problem. Thus, one should have *first hand* knowledge of their programs.

THE MISSION OF THE CHURCH

The mission of the Church, as we have indicated, is not always understood. Is it to save people *from* the world—to save them from the corrupted life of the inner city—or is it to redeem the world? As sacramental, incarnational Christians, we believe it to be the latter. The Church in the inner city must push herself into every aspect of the city's life. What is not taken on cannot be redeemed. The Church can only condemn the role of cultural oasis in a crude social setting, of white society in an integrated neighborhood, of aseptic settlement houses in gangland, or of Bach in rock n' roll. The Church must become incarnate; she must identify as far as possible with the culture of the city and the people of the city. This means an aggressive evangelism, a courageous social action, and a willingness to suffer. It also means a willingness to support the effort on the part of the diocese, district, or presbytery, which must be convinced of this mission and understand the criticism which it may entail.

The mission of each parish should be a concern of a department at a higher level; this applies to emphasis on race relations in a changing neighborhood, attempts to relate to Bohemia in Greenwich Village, concern for labor in parts of Detroit, and the street-gang ministry on the Lower East Side of New York. Each congregation should have its mission described in terms of its setting, its facilities, its leadership, and its resources. Each parish should be helped to see and understand its mission, even if this be to go gracefully out of existence.

SUPPLY

The supply for the troops must be provided by the higher echelon. If a congregation should be self-supporting, it is the presbytery's responsibility to see that proper measures are taken to achieve this goal. In another case, a parish may need help to sustain the extreme pastoral burden of inner-city work. The diocese must furnish such help either directly or by encouraging wealthier parishes to adopt a particular weak parish. One of the heaviest drains upon the morale of the city minister is the uncertainty of his financial status. Lay leadership may also be provided tactfully by other churches in a district to help revive the dying structure of a downtown situation. They may also furnish athletic equipment, clothes, food, furniture, and other essentials.

COMMUNICATION

Here we have the most important and the most neglected aspect of the ministry to the city.

(a) *Communication of clergy with each other.* Without exception, every successful urban work with which I am familiar has had at its center a community of leadership. In the Episcopal Church, for example, this has taken various forms: a team ministry of clergy, their wives, and a religious order (Jersey City); a team ministry of clergy, members of religious orders, wives, lay professional workers (Trinity, New York); traditional rector and associates with a sense of community among them (St. Philip's, Harlem); ministers from separate parishes having a weekly corporate communion (Roxbury, Massachusetts); an enlarged, urban-oriented Cathedral Chapter including the bishop and dean (Indianapolis); or a militant group of laymen working with the ministers.

This community life is essential if the clergy morale is to be sustained and if the guidance of the Holy Spirit is to be received. Such community can also be established across church lines, as in the Indianapolis inner-city minister's fellowship, the East Harlem Protestant Parish, or the West St. Louis Ecumenical Parish.

(b) *Communication of the clergy and the diocese, district, or presbytery.* Besides the pastoral relationship that urban clergy especially need, there should be a committee or department of the higher echelon with urban work as its special concern. This has been handled in a variety of ways; either as a separate structure directly responsible to the bishop or to the overseer, whatever his title, or as a division of a Department of Christian Social Relations or of a Department of Missions. However structured, it is absolutely essential that there be a vigorous group on the level of diocese, district, or presbytery with urban work as its sole concern.

(c) *Communications with the national church.* It is also absolutely essential that a comparable division exist on the national level to act as a center and clearing house for information and research and as a gadfly and source of enthusiasm for the church at large. The pattern that was suggested at the last General

Convention of the Episcopal Church might well be a serviceable one for any church regardless of its structure. That pattern called for a core staff at national headquarters consisting of a chief executive officer, a research man and communicator to gather and disseminate available information through statements, bulletins, tracts for the laity, magazine articles, books, and conference material; and there would be an assistant executive officer with special responsibility for field workers. In the field, there is to be a number of workers to stimulate interest in creative urban work, to show local officials how to set up urban committees or departments, where to find local resources, and to provide any needed assistance. The field workers would also set up conferences at all levels as a means of continually stimulating the church and propagandizing it with the "gospel of urban work."

Without such concern at the national level, the progress of urban work will continue to be spasmodic. At present there are many echelons beyond the parish which have accepted the problem head on and who are doing their best to meet the staggering load of urban responsibility. Such wide-awake organizations would welcome help from any source, I am sure. Other echelons in some of the largest urban areas of the country have not really come to grips with the problem at all. An active and tactful national program could help to awaken these as well as the local parishes to their proper responsibility.

I recently talked to a young priest in a small urban diocese who was very eager to establish an interest in urban work but did not know how to go about it. He could well gather a group of like-minded persons together and with the help of a field worker from the national church go about attaining his goal. Ignorance of method often stands in the way of an effective ministry to urban areas. For instance, a young woman of my acquaintance who had worked as a member of a summer urban program recently moved to a city. She naively approached the clergy of a downtown parish there and asked them what they had done in the neighborhood. The rector said he had done nothing because he did not know what to do. She gave him some concrete suggestions, and now a solid ministry there has begun.

(d) *Communication with other interested agencies.* In addition to the need for interchurch cooperation, the Church also must be related to secular agencies, private and public: courts, probation and parole officials, school systems, and social welfare agencies. These people ordinarily welcome the Church's interest after they overcome their surprise that the Church cares and that the clergy have some technical ability.

This discussion of involvement in urban work has been little more than an outline of some of the important areas for study and action by the diocese, district, or presbytery. There has been no intention to discuss these problems exhaustively; rather, the intention has been to stimulate study and action in an area that is too often neglected.

In conclusion, it should be emphasized that urban work cannot be taken up casually with one's left hand. The Church must enter upon it with a high seriousness, fully aware not only of the glorious opportunities for service and evangelism, but also of the great cost of such an enterprise—cost not only in terms of money, but in terms of embarrassing social involvement and of what is often a suffering sense of failure. The urban experience has often been a crucifixion; with courageous diocesan or district leadership it can be an experience of resurrection, not only for the urban parishes themselves but for the entire diocese, district, or presbytery.

10. *Indianapolis: A Case Study*
of a Cooperative Ministry

"The Church (it was early decided) was not an organization of sinless men but of sinful, not a union of adepts but of less than neophytes, not of illuminati but of those that sat in darkness. Nevertheless, it carried within it an energy not its own, and knew what it believed about energy."

—CHARLES WILLIAMS

ONE of the most encouraging tendencies of the times is the growing realization that the urban ministry cannot be an effort centered in a single parish. As a result, many cooperative ministries are springing up. The following account of one such inner-city ministry, that of the Episcopal Church in Indianapolis, is intended as a sample of the kind of thing which can be attempted. Since it illustrates some of the principles of cooperation we have already discussed, we shall examine it at the risk of some repetition. While it is true that the Indianapolis situation contained some factors which enabled the project to move into operation more quickly and perhaps more effectively than might be expected elsewhere, none of them were such that their absence would preclude a similar operation.

Indianapolis is a midwestern capital city containing large and
small industry and a great many insurance companies, in addition to the apparatus of state government. The city is changing
from a small town to a metropolitan area, and the growing pains
are evident. It is still influenced in its point of view by its heritage
as the center of a farming community.

"Hoosiers" are a proud people and have reason to be; they
have done much on their own and have a history of being, as
they might put it, "solidly American." This pride in Americanism,
however, has its negative aspects and perhaps prevents the kind
of imaginative adaptation which the 1960's demand. Such conservative influences as the national headquarters of the American
Legion, a strong Masonic life, and a conservative Republican
party led by such men as Senator Jenner have stabilized the
community, but in the minds of some these influences have led
to the neglect of such problems as seem to demand outside help.
There is only one public housing project in the city, and it is the
only one in the country, I believe, which has never been accepted
and administered by the municipality. Other more conservative
or even reactionary groups find an audience in Indianapolis: the
John Birch Society was founded there and the morning and
evening papers are, I think one could safely say, hyperconserva-
tive.

The spirit of the community, and therefore of the Church, is
rather suspicious of progress and leery of anything which might
seem "liberal." Expressing the social concern of the Church in
other than rather paternalistic terms has often been difficult and
has met some resistance. On the other hand, Indiana is a strong
church community with an above-average clerical leadership in
both Protestant and Roman Catholic churches. Indianapolis
people are traditionally loyal to their churches and there is a
deep fund of good will available to the work of the church. The
city's population of roughly 500,000 is rapidly increasing. The

Negro population is around 20 per cent and also increasing rapidly. A great many mountain people from Kentucky and Tennessee have come there looking for work.

The center of Indianapolis is Monument Circle, the hub of a wheel-shaped city plan modeled on Washington, D.C. The inner city stretches roughly twenty blocks in each direction, with a typical core of commerce, entertainment, public buildings, and high-rise apartments, surrounded by a blighted area of ghettos containing Negroes and mountain people. This blight edges through a transitional area into suburbs graded out to the very expensive split-level developments typical of postwar America.

The Church Federation is well-run, having an especially effective Division of Research and Planning. The Health and Welfare Council is also active and competent. As in many small cities, one or two families or groups of families have given leadership to charitable and cultural concerns.

The Episcopal Church has long been in Indianapolis, but until recently it ministered only to its own and was almost unknown to the mainstream of Indiana life. People know the "Church on the Circle" (Christ Church Cathedral), but only a rare passer-by could tell one the denomination of this familiar landmark. In the late 1940's, there were three strong parishes on Meridian Street from the circle to 57th Street—the inner-city parishes of St. Philip's (Negro), All Saints' (traditionally Anglo-Catholic), and St. George's (established as a "mill-chapel" by Christ Church at the turn of the century). The only other parish was St. Matthew's in the suburb of Irvington on the east side.

The present bishop, the Rt. Rev. John P. Craine, was called as rector of Christ Church on the Circle in 1949. His ministry, prior to his election as diocesan bishop, consisted of strengthening the parish life of Christ Church, which had been torn by internal controversy, remodeling the plant, and establishing a strong parish organizational life. He became involved in community affairs, and gave a great deal of time to diocesan work. He set the stage for the resurgence of life in the inner-city parishes. He was instrumental in the calling to Christ Church (which had recently become the Cathedral) of a dean whose major concern had been the work of the Church in the inner city, and in calling a part-time director of Christian Social Relations who also would serve the inner-city parish of All Saints'. The bishop had long visualized a cooperative ministry in the city: he delegated the work to the new men, backing them every step of the way and giving them the benefit of his intimate knowledge of the city and his own long experience in urban work.

INVOLVEMENT AND IMAGE-CHANGING

The inner-city program was conceived in a broad context: the impact of the Episcopal Church on the city as a whole and the gradual change of her *image* from a conservative, quiet, socially elite church to one deeply concerned with the problems of the total life of the city. The working out of this plan has been one of the most fascinating aspects of the recent history of the diocese. On the one hand, the respect for the Episcopal Church has risen tremendously among that relatively small group of persons who are deeply aware of the social problems of the city: social workers, some politicians, leaders of minority groups, clergy of other denominations, and leaders. On the other hand, there has been a sense of betrayal on the part of many more conservative Episcopalians who have never been exposed to the Church's involvement in "worldly" affairs and who feel very strongly that the Church has no business there.

Crises arise from time to time over such issues as the bitter "Right to Work" battle, the religious factor of the presidential campaign with its strong emotional content, or the question of race relations. Some of the laity have withdrawn financial support, and a few have left the Church. Others have, I believe, gone along with the hope that this would be only a passing phase. Some have gradually been widening their vision to include this part of the ministry; still others are thrilled and excited by the developments. However, the resentment of some of the wealthier members has to some extent hampered the financing of social outreach. It has been hard to separate in people's minds the social *service* of the Church, harmless even to the most reactionary and in line with the Hoosier philosophy that private agencies (including the Church) are responsible for welfare problems, and the social action and prophetic ministry of the Church as expressed through the Department of Christian Social Relations. Prophetic and pastoral—the eternal conflict!

The techniques of community involvement and image-changing have included the apportioning by the bishop of fields of social concern to various clergy and laymen so the Church would have a voice, officially or unofficially, in diverse aspects of the life of the city. The CSR executive takes charge of labor and mental health; the Cathedral dean, Human Relations, Planned Parenthood, the Church Federation Division of Research, and cooperation in the inner-city area; the bishop deals with alcoholism on the state level and the Health and Welfare Council. The clergy have been involved in a variety of television and radio programs, and the diocesan newspaper has been reinvigorated; these and other means of communication are being explored continually.

The germination of the Urban Mission Program occurred in the weekly Tuesday morning meetings and corporate Communions of the inner-city and diocesan clergy. The Cathedral Chapter serves in the role of advisor to the dean and bishop in regard to the policy and operation of the Cathedral. (The authority of the Cathedral *parish* is similar to the traditional rector-vestry relationship.) Chapter meetings were enlarged to include the clergy of the inner-city parishes and the director of the Episcopal Community Services. Other interested clergy were always welcome. Thus the Chapter became a Christian community around the bishop, who customarily celebrated the Eucharist preceding an informal breakfast. Out of the warm and sometimes good-naturedly turbulent meeting which followed, the hopes and plans for the urban mission of the Church developed.

The plans and techniques of urban work are secondary to the spirit and theological concern behind it; this spirit and a deep incarnational concern flowed naturally from the Eucharistic base of the Chapter meetings and from the humor and friendship of those involved. These continue to grow deeper as the years go by. Frictions were worked out here, sunken morales boosted, and delicate problems of human relations resolved. The bishop also found this a trusted and sympathetic community with whom he could discuss his hopes, dreams, and fears.

Whatever form the inner-city work was to take, it was clear that the Cathedral parish had to be convinced that it was worthwhile. Thus, parallel to the formation and planning of the Chapter, a self-study plan was instituted in the Cathedral during Lent of 1958. Over a hundred and forty persons participated in this Bible-study-centered examination. Two results were clear: all who participated experienced some widening of their understanding of what the Church is and what her vocation in the city could be; thirty or forty persons found themselves ready to begin to bring a change into being. These laymen launched a neighborhood program on a parish level in an area ten blocks from the Cathedral. It soon became clear that even this distance, measured in psychological terms, was impassable. To bridge this gap, the experimental "Cathedral House" ministry was undertaken, using an old house as a neighborhood base. The other parishes also were working with their people; the groundwork was being laid.

Another work of the Spirit was the establishment at this time of a special endowment within the Cathedral financial structure, the income of which could revert to the Cathedral for salaries or even for rebuilding the plant if this should become necessary. Meanwhile, the income was to be used for any religious purpose in the city except the current expenses of the Cathedral parish. A committee of clergy and laymen representing the diocese and the parish was authorized to allocate the funds. The spirit of this endowment was to make advance and experimental work of a missionary and/or welfare nature possible in the present and to insure the financial structure of the Cathedral in the future without threatening the present healthy stewardship of the membership at large.

At this point one might say, "No wonder they can do these fine things in Indianapolis; they have a special fund and a small diocese." These are indeed special factors. However, I am convinced that with prayer, effort, and imagination similar kinds of financing are much more possible elsewhere than is generally acknowledged. There have been tremendous endowments built up over the years for church music, church settlement houses, old ladies homes, and the like. If the laity can be converted to a sense of the urgency of urban work, the financing will come. Even without it, a humble beginning can be made. A program in action brings response more quickly than a vague desire to do something. Furthermore, a breakthrough in inexpensive urban mission work is bound to come sooner or later. The endowment has been the source of funds for the urban program, the establishment of an Episcopal bookstore, and assistance to the fledgling Episcopal Community Services, a church casework agency. It is to be noted that the diocese is thus relieved of the claims of the Urban Mission and may concentrate elsewhere. This is a mixed blessing, for it also meant that the diocese as a whole was not being educated to the same extent as if it were footing the bills. Just recently it has begun contributing.

An Urban Mission Council, composed of the rector and two laymen from each inner-city parish, was established. This group was to be the official policy council for all cooperative ventures, all neighborhood work, and all financing of these efforts. Also, a gentleman's agreement was made to clear with the Council any radical departures in the parish work of any of the participating parishes. The internal canonical authority of each parish was carefully preserved, to avoid any threat to traditional prerogatives or the danger of the Cathedral parish's establishing a condescending relationship toward the others. This Council has since been incorporated and has executive responsibility for the inner-city program. The Cathedral Chapter is now advisory to the Council.

One of the ticklish problems in this stage of the work was the administrative aspect. In addition to the urban work, the diocese was busy initiating an active Department of Christian Social Relations (CSR) and the Episcopal Community Services (ECS), after having recently added an old people's home and a bookstore and enlarged the Department of Missions. Yet the diocese was still relatively small, and the staff leadership thin; an attempt had to be made to visualize the administrative future best fashioned to advance the purposes of each effort. At the same time duplication or fussy busy work had to be avoided, for many of the clergy and laymen found themselves on several boards. Furthermore, ECS and CSR were domiciled in the same building, the inadequate parish house of All Saints' Church. In the final structure the bishop is ex-officio chairman of each, and the president does the active work; this arrangement safeguards the Church's interest in the endeavor over the years. Other subdivisions are merely committees. All report through the CSR department to the Bishop and Council.

The organizational aspect has been described in some detail because it is at this level that so many church endeavors founder. They are either inadequately organized so that they fall apart with the wind, or they are so cumbersome that vigorous and imaginative work is impossible. One particular principle should be stressed: the parish-centered, evangelistic work of the inner city should be completely separate organizationally from the casework, the social welfare work of the Church, although they work in closest cooperation. Each work is staffed differently and requires completely different skills; a proper view of Church social work should divorce any overt evangelism from the ministry of help. Problems can be avoided at the parish grass roots if people can be referred to the church agency rather than given material aid on the spot. Moreover, the new people reached through urban evangelism come into the Body of Christ as equals and in no way should be tagged as "charity cases." In organizing the Indianapolis work, the principle of clarity of purpose with a minimum of organization needed to do the work has been followed; lay ministry at the leadership level has also been encouraged.

SURVEYING THE RESULTS

Having described the over-all structure, let us examine briefly the effect the program has had in each of the parishes.

CHRIST CHURCH CATHEDRAL

Since the initiation of the self-study program, the understanding of the parish has grown on many levels, as has the clergy's respect for the deep dedication of the laity. In this section, however, I shall deal only with the specialized ministry of Cathedral House. The heart of this ministry has been the leadership of the laymen. Not only have they put in endless hours of work, but it is they who have made the decisions, good and bad, which have built the work into a solid and enduring enterprise.

After the impracticality of neighborhood work from the Cathedral building itself became apparent, the Social Relations Committee of the parish began a search for a nearby house. A ramshackle one was rented for the exorbitant fee of $100 a month. Some people felt that the parish should renovate or build a "decent clean structure." Others, who won the day, felt that doing so would erect an additional barrier in the work, and that the house should blend into the neighborhood as much as possible. After a year's use, the house looked worse than any other in the block!

The program began with a recreation ministry to the children, to which was added, by degrees, religious education. In each the basic theme was the ministry of love, filling the sometimes desperate emotional, physical, and spiritual needs of the children in the name of Christ. No *quid pro quo* was demanded; many children continued to attend the Baptist Church or no church. But the work continues, and after four years the parents are finally being touched. In the summer, two or three full-time helpers are present; in the winter the program is an evening one manned by volunteers under the direction of a part-time lay worker, supervised by one of the Cathedral clergy. A "new" house is now owned, and the year 1960-61 marked the acceptance by the Cathedral vestry of Cathedral House as more than a momentary endeavor.

Perhaps the most basic problem is the relationship of the Cathedral House neighborhood people to the parish itself. The theory is that they will be full members of the parish who worship there on Sunday and that Cathedral House itself will be a weekday place for activity, fellowship, and weekday worship. At present, some of the children come to the Cathedral and enter into the Sunday School and other activities. One little girl walked twenty blocks in the snow to be present when she missed her ride one morning. Whether the full-scale incorporation of many neighborhood people envisioned by this plan is but a dream remains to be seen.

Another difficulty faced by the project is the relationship of the lay workers to the people they serve at Cathedral House. They come from another cultural level out of a sense of being needed by the people in the neighborhood. There is a danger of paternalism resulting from the lack of identification between suburban Christians and the residents of a blighted area. However, all things are possible in Christ. On the surface, such crossing of cultural lines may look like only a neurotic outlet or a conscience-salving activity for odd laymen. On the surface many mixed motivations may be present on the part of those who do the work. Nonetheless, over the long missionary history of the Church our Lord often has been brought from one culture to another through the work of the Spirit and the ministry of Christian love. Identification has taken place. Perhaps deeper friendships have been formed across the barriers of culture than within them, for when the love is strong enough to break those barriers it is strong indeed. We pray that continued sincere work and prayer will create true communication in the Spirit.

The Cathedral recently has launched a special three-year "research" ministry into the problems peculiar to reaching people who live and work in the core of downtown. A full time clergyman is engaged in this work under the direction of the Dean and an advisory committee of laymen.

ALL SAINTS'

Here a true sense of parish vocation is coming into being in spite of tension and struggle. Here, in one small house, are lodged the Episcopal Community Services, the Department of Christian Social Relations, and the parish of All Saints'. (A new headquarters and parish house is being built with diocesan funds.) Many of the same personnel work in more than one capacity and in more than one of these entities. The director of ECS is also assistant to the rector of the parish, who in turn is the diocesan CSR executive. The confusion of the laity by these organizations is reminiscent of early New Deal days in Washington! But despite some justifiable confusion and frustration the parish is changing, taking upon itself the difficult task of being landlord to the two agencies, reaching out into the neighborhood as part of the Urban Mission Council program, and still maintaining its traditional high level of Anglo-Catholic liturgical practice. This transformation is due largely to the geniality, understanding, and loving concern of a rector who will not budge from the principles of Christian social justice which are his life-blood —and to a small group of extraordinary laymen.

Here is a perfect example of the way in which a beaten inner-city parish can grow in size and depth if given a significant job to do under wise leadership. The most engaging aspect of the work there has been the natural introduction into the full life of the Church of many of the clients of Episcopal Community Service. One said recently, "I wanted to join that Church because I just never saw a place that cared more for the children around here. . . . I just feel beauty and peace when I go into that big church."

ST. PHILIP'S

This is not untypical of the Negro parishes of the Episcopal Church found around the country from Chicago to Miami. It had been neglected by the diocese for years, especially when it most needed help in its early days. In spite of a feeling of being orphaned, the hard core of loyal laymen has remained. However, their energies had been so aimed at the preservation of the parish (for where else would they go in Indianapolis of twenty years ago?) that until recently evangelism and neighborhood concern were almost ignored. At least no long-range parish involvement in the neighborhood was developing.

Suffice it to say that the breakthrough at St. Philip's has been as hard if not harder than those at the Cathedral and All Saints'. The rector has sensed new support from the inclusion of his parish in the total program of the inner city, and many of his people rejoice at the growing ministry there. But the people are involved in what is often a wearing struggle in their own private lives. The Church for them has been, in a sense, an island away from struggle. Therefore it is hard to generate enthusiasm and to enlist volunteers from those who live away from the neighborhood and who, like so many other churchmen, would prefer to separate themselves from the inner city which they left years ago after much hard work. But the rector and a nucleus of laymen have bravely persevered in making an impact on the surroundings, and the inner vitality of the parish is increasing. St. Philip's program has been most successful in some respects; its potential is perhaps higher than that of the other inner-city parishes, if the long years of distrust and discouragement can eventually be completely overcome. The parish has recently bought an apartment house next door to use in its expanding program.

Just over the horizon lies another opportunity for St. Philip's; the Medical Center of Indiana University is expanding in its direction. Some day this parish may well have a new vocation: ministry to that huge community of hospitals and students. Here is another lesson for the inner city: neighborhoods overnight may become something quite different from what they were. The diocese must insist on at least a holding operation in certain locations, so that the opportunity of future ministry will not be lost.

ST. GEORGE'S

This church is now closed. Although it was originally part of the combined urban program with a promising short-term goal, it soon became clear that the long-term ministry there would dissolve. Surveys and advice were sought from the local Church Federation office and from the National Council Division on Urban Work. The projection showed increasing industrialization and finally the severance of an already small isolated pocket by a throughway. Furthermore, the Presbyterians had had a long and heavily subsidized ministry nearby and were anxious to include St. George's Church in their operation. With funds limited, it seemed that the only logical course was to close the parish and look to some future work on the south side in a location of our choice. The ending of a parish's life is always a sad thing; yet if all factors point in that direction, courage to kill is necessary and preferable to the agony of slow death.

There is nothing extraordinary about the above account, and one hopes that it describes only the beginning. Factors have been favorable in many ways, but one of the reasons for this is that a few people have been concerned, have begun to build, and have steadily prayed for the success of the work.

11. *Ecumenical Urban Ventures*

"It is between our ignorances that our courteous Lord might cause exchange to lie, till the exchange itself became an invocation of the adorable Spirit who has so often deigned to instruct and correct the Church by voices without as well as within the Church."

—CHARLES WILLIAMS

As THE ecumenical movement gathers momentum at the top, it is not strange that it begins to come to life at the grass roots, especially where the Church has her back against the wall in a missionary situation. The general reasons for ecumenicity in the inner city are the same as those for unity in the Church of South India. Churchmen are a tiny minority; traditional Christendom is strange to the culture. There is little strength for a mighty task.

The clergy and lay leaders in the city are more and more thinking and acting like missionaries, realizing that the Church at present is not geared to its inner-city job. They are reaching out for new techniques. They are establishing agencies to deal with social problems which are beyond the individual parish's ability to solve, just as foreign missionaries build hospitals and other institutions. They band together to better finance their programs and seek funds of wealthy parishes and the upper echelons of their denominations, just as missionaries have done for centuries.

It is not strange, then, that these workers also seek to cooperate on an interchurch basis. Several types of cooperation are being tried, and they will be discussed here.

ORGANIC UNITY

The first great experiment in organic unity was the East Harlem Protestant Parish.[1] The parish had its origins in the postwar generation of Union Seminary, the theologically sophisticated interdenominational seminary near Columbia University in New York. Don Benedict, one of the organizers, had experienced prison as a C.O. and combat in Iwo Jima. His colleague was Bill Webber, a former naval officer. The third "founder" was Archie Hargraves, a Negro, who had grown up in North Carolina in the depression. Their approach to the work was aggressive and combative. They were impatient with what they considered irrelevancies and wanted to get on with the job.

From the start, the East Harlem Protestant Parish was oriented to social action. In such a lair of corruption and devastation as Puerto Rican Harlem, half-way measures seemed ridiculous. The Christians had to be where decisions were made; they lived in the area, identified with the people, and brought an unvarnished crucified Christ to share the passion of Harlem.

The ecumenicity of the venture seemed almost secondary and completely inevitable, since no essential barrier existed between these Protestants and since their devotion to the work transcended all barriers but the essential ones. The following is an early state-

[1] *See* George W. Webber, *God's Colony in Man's World* (Nashville: Abingdon, 1960); and Bruce Kenrick, *Come Out the Wilderness* (New York: Harper & Row, 1962).

ment of the East Harlem Protestant Parish and two similar ventures which were started on the same pattern:

Preamble to the Basis of Our Unity

We have come together, united in our response to the love of God, who was in Christ reconciling the world unto Himself. Our continuing unity comes from God, Who has brought us together, and Who has called us to minister unto His people who sit in darkness in the depressed inner-city areas of our civilization. Our work begins and goes forward in the faith that Jesus Christ is our Lord and Saviour. We find light for our work from the divinely inspired Scriptures and we trust in Christ's promise of the gift of the Holy Spirit to guide and strengthen us as we witness to Him. We recognize His universal Church as the effective instrument for redemption in the world.

Our particular concern is for the evangelization of the masses of men and women in our industrial centers who have been disinherited by society and neglected by the churches. Recognizing present-day Protestantism's difficulties and inadequacies in ministering to these victims of massification, we are concerned, with others of our generation, that there be a constant reformation within Protestantism. We accept the spirit of primitive Christianity and of the Protestant Reformation. We have returned to the Church's partially abandoned strategy of ministering to the people in neighborhoods or areas known as parishes. We have deliberately crossed the man-made boundaries of denomination and race. We seek to work toward God's rule over all of life, toward His redemption of the whole lives of the people of our Parishes, toward the healing of society. Our attempts to reach men with the good news of hope and justice and God's love will continue to carry us into nonconventional church activities, such as: using storefronts and vacant lots for church functions; undertaking community action campaigns which demonstrate Christ's continuing concern, through His Church, for man's health and welfare; fighting for justice in the economic and political structures of our world in response to God's redemptive purposes.

As individuals, we have committed ourselves to this kind of ministry as fully as possible, though we do not exclude the possibility that at some future time our concerns may spread our work into other areas in which needs are not being met by modern Protestantism. We have bound ourselves together into local parish Group Ministries in which our members not only share this common basic commitment but also accept devotional, vocational, economic, and political group disciplines which we feel will serve to strengthen our work. We believe that such Group Ministries will enable us:

1. To make an effective, united approach to neglected people.
2. To mutually support and criticize one another's work in a central group of committed individuals.
3. To develop strategies with the benefit of a variety of minds.
4. To witness to a Christian idea of community.

In order to unite and enhance the work of our existing parishes, in order to refine our purposes and our strategies with the benefit of wider experience and participation, in order to stimulate a greater Christian witness in the inner-city areas of other industrial centers we have now created an inter-city council of the Group Ministries of our local parishes.

We dedicate the efforts of this council to the glory of God and to the work of His Church. Although we feel there are real unique features about our mission, our intention is to remain actively within the historic Church. Our spirit is ecumenical rather than separatistic. We recognize our dependence upon the total Church for support, and we invite the criticism and suggestions of this full community of Christians upon our work. We are cognizant of the place of human sin and weakness in even our best efforts. Our greatest hope is that God may choose to correct and guide our work and use it in some way, however small, in His redemptive purposes for all His children.

The sense of community in the parish was intense. Each participant took on basic disciplines. *Devotional:* There were daily prayers, a home worship center, and group worship. *Vocational:* The individual was to make vocational decisions only after consultation with the group. *Health:* One full day off a week was included. (Neglect of this principle has been the downfall of many urban clergy.) *Study:* Three hours a week and group study of one book every month was the norm. *Political:* Group decision was made on local political issues. *Economic:* The staff was paid according to need and economic index.

The Church organization stated that the parish was made up of "free" churches of the non-episcopal tradition. Standards of membership, classes for admission, liturgical standards, and Bible study were essentials of their life together. One of the four cooperating congregations was Presbyterian; the other three operated like a "community church." All members of all congregations were also members of the Parish at large.[2]

The East Harlem parish has done most effective work and has established counterparts in New Haven, Cleveland, and Chicago. The basic strength of its communication has been the participants' deep dedication and the clergy's ability to sacrifice their middle-class ways and superficial values to the mission of Christ. The parish has been strong in witness—a life-size "Passion Play" on Good Friday in a vacant lot is typical of its imaginative methods. It has been strong in social action and community life.

On the other hand, there have been some problems in evangelism—in terms of actual church membership—and in liturgy. (Most Episcopalians, for example, are dubious of a special liturgy for a specific parish.) There have been other built-in problems, such as those which arise when a member moves away. Like the French priest worker's followers, the East Harlem parishioners, accustomed to an ecumenical yet a ceremonial and socially concerned parish, may not feel at home elsewhere. This parish is not founding a denomination, yet something of a tendency in this direction persists. The size of the staff sometimes seems excessive, and one would imagine that the financial burden is heavy.

[2] This review of principles is taken from a conference work sheet dated 1952.

In spite of these weaknesses, however, the heroic witness of the East Harlem Protestant Parish over fifteen years has had a greater impact on the urban work of Protestantism in America than any other venture and has helped to shape Protestant movements of rebirth in the inner city along socially concerned lines. Its ecumenical success perhaps is due to its lack of self-consciousness—the work comes first, the ecumenicity follows.

In Cleveland, one of the participating parishes is an Episcopal Church. As is the case with the Presbyterian Church in East Harlem, its members fulfill obligations of their own church discipline, as well as participate as members of the parish at large, subject to its responsibilities and privileges.

FEDERATION

The West St. Louis Ecumenical Parish is part of a large ecumenical venture between Presbyterians and Episcopalians on many levels. The "Parish" includes eleven churches: two are Episcopal, two Presbyterian U.S., two United Presbyterian U.S.A., two Methodist, one colored Methodist Episcopal, one Congregational, and one African Methodist Episcopal. This effort is in its early stages. There is great theological freedom; one of the Episcopal churches is Anglo-Catholic by tradition, and at the other extreme is the Congregational parish.

Unlike the East Harlem Protestant Parish, there is no corporate discipline, and there is a corresponding lack of corporate intensity. The East Harlem venture began pretty much from nothing, whereas the St. Louis project is a joint venture of old established churches which have seen better days. The eleven ministers have pledged to keep their congregations in the inner city, where they are. They have agreed to pool their experience, creativity, personnel, finances, and buildings. A Parish Assembly contains four representatives from each parish. It is the parish's aim to improve the living conditions of the area and also to bring people to Christ. The various participants cooperate in social action and their first major joint project, a vigorous campaign against illiteracy in the area, has been a great success. Their access to University help in this program points to resources which often are available but unused in the inner city. Great promise lies ahead in cooperation with the Church Federation in long-range planning.

It is too early to judge the full effectiveness of this effort. It probably will never have the hot dynamic of East Harlem, but it is more "reproducible" in most typical inner-city situations across the country.

ORGANIZED COOPERATION

Still another type of ecumenical venture is being undertaken in an Indianapolis project known as Operation "Prove It." While this project is not yet fully in operation, it is discussed here as an example of a third possible form of ecumenical activity: cooperation on an organized basis in some part of the program of each supporting church.

This project is under the general sponsorship of the Church Federation. It will be supervised by a board representative of all the participating churches, and each of the ten neighborhood churches directly involved and each in adjacent areas will have the backing of its own denominational authorities. Employing conventional and experimental techniques, Operation "Prove It" will attempt to answer the contention of both friendly and unfriendly critics that in decaying areas of our central cities the Church has not been displaying any great aptitude for completing her mission.

The social services are to be completely shared, with each parish shouldering responsibility for that part of the work for which it is best equipped, whether that be adult groups, gym programs, or casework. However, the worship and membership of the persons reached will be according to their own choice, and no attempt at ecumenicity on the level of organic Church life is to be made.

The target area is a well-defined twenty-block section of the inner city. Among the first steps is a detailed census designed to provide basic demographic data and insights into the social and religious climate. The mere fact of taking such a census expresses the concern of the Church for the inhabitants; its repetition will later provide an evaluation of the effectiveness of the program. Of course, many feel that such a census is virtually a waste of time because of the rapid changes of residence and because of the human tendency to feel the job is done when the census is complete. Another source of information feed-back would be the professionals released part time from their church and secular agencies to work with complete freedom in the area. If an existing church chooses to experiment with Boy Scout groups, day care centers, special interest clubs, or centers for the aged that would be encouraged. So too would such denominational projects as attempting to start a new indigenous church or the extension of the program of the Episcopal Cathedral House.

If this program is to succeed the great bulk of the work will of necessity be done by laymen. They will take the census, plan programs, man centers, do calling, and serve as teachers and counselors in many types of situations. These laymen will be not only those in the area directly concerned, but also those from other sections of the city whose churches will also provide financial support for Operation "Prove It." It may well be that the work of the inner-city Church depends upon the ability of these lay people to identify with the problems of other people and find in the gospel the incentive to forget class and privilege. These laymen may well learn about "picking up the Cross" in this attempt to save the churches in the inner city. The plan seems valid, but as yet no real dynamic has developed; a wait and see attitude is in order.

This brief survey of three ecumenical approaches to the inner city is a mere sampling with which the author is familiar. Other experiments are going on elsewhere on many levels and will increase unless the climate alters radically. There are lines of tension within an organization loose enough to allow the Episcopal Church, for example, to live a penetrating liturgical life and yet firm enough to create a vibrant and intense community life, so necessary if we are to cut sharply into the amorphous mass of disorganized life and death in the inner city. The danger of the wrong kind of ecumenicity would be the watering down of an already tepid Protestantism in order to forward the superorganization of an already overorganized Church. Such watering down opens the way to a subtle takeover by secularism in the form of social work techniques without the theology to undergird them.

It would seem that vigor must be intensified in the individual parish, which, as a vigorous *unit*, would cooperate with other vigorous *units* so that they would complement, not conflict with, each other. Or there must be a radical union like the East Harlem Protestant Parish where the vigor is intensified in the over-all community. "Finding a middle ground" might jeopardize liveliness in either the individual unit or the over-all parish.

Another possible conflict lies within the ethos of each tradition. It is difficult to work effectively with Christians from an almost completely different tradition who think, feel, and pray so differently that they give one goose pimples. When the work is hard anyway, one shrinks back from another burden in the center of the source of strength. Yet our Lord commands us to be one; where better can our groping toward unity take place than among Christ's brothers in the inner city?

12. The Parish and Social Work

"One cannot love downwards, de haut en bas. *That is reserved for God. One cannot love when one thinks oneself superior—even if one is superior. Human love is always between equals."*

—CHARLES WILLIAMS

THE Church had developed her own science of the cure of souls at one time. It was a complete science and consisted of the best methods then known for treating people's emotional and spiritual problems. Among the clergy were technicians skilled in this work. Thus a person in trouble, when he came to the Church, received the best help available. There were then, as there are today, incompetent clergy, and some of the principles of early pastoral theology would make a psychiatrist's hair stand on end. Nevertheless, no better assistance was obtainable.

Now the situation is different. Modern science has developed an elaborate set of techniques for treating both the physical and the emotional problems of human beings. Also it has demonstrated scientifically what the Church has always known—that the two are inextricably related. This means that the "spiritual" cure of souls has been cut off, in practice, from physical and emotional therapy. The most effective treatment of the human person can no longer be claimed for pastoral techniques unaided by the skills which have been developed in the secular disciplines of medicine, psychiatry, and social work. In this chapter, we will discuss the Church's developing role as she comes to grips with this situation, examining the implications in the areas of theology, technique, and witness to the community.

In the inner city, and particularly in the "blighted areas," the clergyman is involved continually in relationships with private and public social agencies. He also must deal with a wider range of concern than his fellow pastor in suburbia or uptown. His people come to him not only with the problems usually thought to be within his province as a clergyman, but also with many others which require the techniques of social work for their solution. Thus it is essential for the inner-city pastor to understand the discipline of social work.

THEOLOGY AND THE PSYCHIATRIC APPROACH

Generally speaking, social work theory is based upon the findings of psychology and psychiatry. Since in some parts of the Church these disciplines are still suspect, it seems wise to briefly examine their theological implications. There is no basic conflict between the insights of depth psychology in its non-technical sense and Christian doctrine. Beginning with its attitude toward Galileo, the Church has too often rejected scientific insight, when it first appears, as being at odds with the Church's current understanding of the nature of some aspect of reality. When the new knowledge appears to be here to stay, the Church begins to wrestle with its implications and finds, after much soul searching, that the conflict is only with certain interpretations of God's truth, not with the truth itself. Galileo, Darwin, Freud—the story is the same with each.

Without examining in detail the different schools of psychology and their relation to the Christian doctrine of man, it can be noted that common to them all is the basic insight that man has an "unconscious" which deeply affects his conscious behavior. This does not contradict the Christian understanding of man's nature; in fact, the Christian view gives added and useful aids to the therapist, be he psychiatrist, social worker, or priest.

Man is made in the image of God. This truth undergirds the drive to health commented on so often in descriptions of the therapeutic process. Without it, of course, there would be no motivation on the part of the patient and no hope on the part of the therapist, since all cure must have as its driving force the desire of the patient to be well and the general tendency of the mind toward health.

Man is also a fallen creature. Here we have the theological basis for such observable phenomena as introversion and ambivalence toward the self. One of the principal aims of therapy is to turn one away from oneself toward healthy relationships with others and with God.

Yet man *has been redeemed* by the love of Christ, who suffered and died for him, and *is being redeemed and can only be redeemed* by love. This fact is obviously related to the emotional role of the therapist in regard to acceptance, transference, and the absorption of hostility while maintaining acceptance and concern. The therapist is acting out the principles of redemption demonstrated on the Cross. Consciously or unconsciously, he is using the Grace of God which operates through all human love and which is present in the world only because of the cosmic change in the nature of reality brought about for all eternity by the action of God through Christ upon the Cross.

Finally, our religion is a sacramental religion; we who profess to believe in the Holy Catholic Church reiterate that the physical is good (God made it) and that God works through physical things (as Christ's human flesh, the Bread and Wine). On this belief is based a healthy doctrine of the physical side of man's nature (including sex, so important in therapy) and a willingness of the Church to *use* secular techniques as vehicles of the Grace of God.

It is along lines such as these that theology informs the therapeutic process and learns from it as well. Perhaps the tendency has been to let it end there, as though the Church has heaved a sigh of relief to know that Freud has not completely discredited her hard-won place in society. But we are beginning to see the mutual deepening these two disciplines can give to each other. It is the duty of those involved to continue to roll back the mysteries of the human person, finding in the richness of God breadths of healing hitherto unsuspected and using the sharp knife of scientific technique to cut away lazy apprehension, sentimentality, and subjective emotionalism of the wrong kind. Thus the clear power of Deity can be brought to bear with full force upon the disturbed human psyche.

TECHNIQUE IN COUNSELING

As Christians we believe that the ultimate healer is God and that the healing of one human being by another is a channel of this power, mediated through love, reason, and skill. The person-to-person relationship in healing is a combination of God's healing power and the human freedom to use that part of our destiny over which God has delegated to us the control. There is an area in and around the three-sided relationship of patient, therapist, and God which as yet has not been fully explored. Too many priests forget their priestliness when they learn some of the basic skills of counseling—or perhaps they have not been trained properly in the use of priestly techniques and therefore are not confident in their exercise. These clergy become "clinical therapists" who happen to have the prefix "reverend" in front of their name.

Many trained social workers and psychiatrists do not even dream of looking into the Church's treasury of healing; many clergymen best trained in priestly arts eschew any reliance at all upon the psychiatric. This divorce between body and soul even invades the Church's pastoral ministry. As a result, consciously allowing the patient to make his transference to God in the therapeutic process is rare in counseling. Granted, the therapist must be at first the person to whom the patient relates. Ultimately, however, no matter how adjusted the patient becomes, for his health, independent security, and final salvation, he must relate to the Person of God.

THE CHURCH AND THE PROFESSION OF SOCIAL WORK

The counseling process is but a small part of casework. The relationship of the Church as an institution to the profession of social work must also be considered.

Our Lord Jesus Christ reached out to heal the man with the unclean spirit in the synagogue at Capernaum, and the man asked, "What have we to do with Thee, Jesus, thou Nazarene?" Ever since then the Church has felt impelled to go forth and heal in the name of that same Christ. As Jesus' teaching and the Church's understanding of it deepened, even more profound reasons for the healing ministry came to light. Not only did he command us to heal and help in imitation of him, but he assured us that in so doing we were actually ministering to him. Down through the ages Christians have found him there in those who suffer, as surely as they found him in the Eucharist. They have found also that any Christian spirituality would be a thin and distorted thing if it ceased to meet Christ in his poor—the poor of body, mind, and spirit.

As the Church ministers to those in need she is acting out the work of the Kingdom; she is being true to her essential quality as the Body of Christ. In recent years there has been much discussion of the ministry of the laity. And there is probably no area of the Church's life where the ministry of the laity is more obviously demonstrated than in the social work of the Church. In discussing the philosophy and techniques of social work, let us remember that the workers *are* ministers of the Church as they go about their appointed rounds, just as surely as the clergyman in his way fulfills his ministry.

In the year 1956 in this country over six million clients were serviced by social workers in one way or another. Federal and local government, industry, adoption agencies, YMCA's, rehabilitation centers, veterans' associations, and employment agencies used social work to carry out the purpose for which they were established in an increasingly complicated society. The Church also is an institution in a very complicated society. Her purpose is the bringing in of the Kingdom by the ministry of God's love. Should she, of all groups, reject the means of implementing that love? *All* truth is of God, including the esoteric phraseology of social work.

Good will is often not enough to help those who are caught up in the complicated pressures of this society. In fact, good will misdirected can do more harm than good. It is for this reason that the Church, wishing to do the best within her power for those who need her help, enlists the skilled techniques of the social worker to fulfill her ministry of love.

PASTORAL WORK AND CASEWORK

In many parts of the country there is still prejudice against the profession of social work. The unenlightened churchman thinks of social workers as professionals who, because of their devotion to scientific method and because they are on salary, render a service which is cold and impersonal and the very antithesis of love.

There are those who connect social work with the government's interference in the personal lives of people, somehow associating the profession with New Deal ideas and the welfare state. In Indianapolis, for instance, in recent years there has been a concerted effort on the part of certain sections of the press to discredit the integrity and reliability of social workers who are on the city payroll. The press has called for the opening up of clients' files and the divulging of privileged communication which clients have given to caseworkers whom they trusted. On the part of clients, there is a fear of the social worker as a policeman in sheep's clothing who comes into their lives as an arm of authority to manipulate and control.

Such prejudices make many social workers defensive, make them feel that the society which they are seeking to improve is itself against them; thus the effectiveness of their work is impaired. Since, like most prejudices, these are a result of ignorance, let us examine the philosophy of social work to see whether there be any basis at all for these assumptions and prejudices.

The basic aim of social work is to help persons be themselves by assisting them to achieve emotional and social security. By manipulating the environment, by re-education, and by lending strong moral support, the worker helps the client through an impossible situation which has paralyzed and imprisoned him and frees him to become a productive member of the community. The social worker deals with the whole person in terms of his job, his family, his housing, and himself. It is important to say here that without the kind of security which is the aim of social work it is very hard for a person to function as a productive member of society or of the Church.

Social work differs from other ways of helping in that it has a is a thorny question; the Church loathes to say No to someone in need, yet where do we draw the line? One rule of thumb could be that the agency would never handle a case which a priest or an untrained layman could handle just as well. Agency staff members are specialists in delicate counseling problems for which the priest is not equipped and in the use of referral agencies about which the priest is not fully enough informed. The agency must be flexible, but at the same time it must never become so overloaded that it loses professional standing.

CHURCH SOCIAL AGENCY: ITS VOCATION

A church agency does not exist in a vacuum. It exists in a community already occupied by churches and secular agencies, and only in relationship to them can we see the church agency in proper perspective. Moreover, it is only as we see the possibility of creative therapy based on theological insight that we can understand the church agency in its most fundamental role, for it is here that its double heritage can best be integrated.

It is sometimes asked why we need a church agency in a well-organized modern city which already has its Family Service, Child Guidance, Crittenden Homes, State Aid to Dependent Children, and Public Welfare Service. The most obvious answer is that no modern city has enough agencies to meet the quantity of need which urban life produces.

However, the church agency should do more than add to the volume of work being done. It should be more flexible than the secular agencies and should fill the gaps created by the sometimes rigid intake policies of other organizations. It can also, because of its flexibility, be the unifying force in a family bewildered by a multiplicity of services. A recent case at the Episcopal Community Services in Indianapolis was involved with ten separate agencies during the course of a year.

built-in discipline that guards against ulterior motives on the part of the worker. You and I go out to help someone in trouble. We may not consider our motives: the good feeling it gives us inside, the need to feel superior to someone else, the need for someone to be dependent upon us, the wish to project our own ideas of living onto this other person, or the search for new members for the Church.

The social worker, because of his training, watches such tendencies within himself. Being under constant supervision, his motives are scrutinized by a superior. The scientific objectivity of social work insures, as far as is humanly possible, that the good of the client and the community are the only ends being sought. This is the reason, for instance, that adoption agencies seem so exasperating in their elaborate red tape. The very term "client" describes a self-respecting person retaining an agency for his own well-being, as one might retain a lawyer. He is neither a sick "patient" nor someone who is being shepherded toward a particular faith, as a "parishioner."

This austere objectivity might well be studied by the Church in the pastoral area. The clergy and the volunteer should continually judge themselves by these same standards. Christian love is poured out toward another with no ulterior motive except the other's welfare. To the degree that the love is selfish it ceases to be love in the deepest sense of that word. This does not mean that there is nothing for the Church to teach social work in return. Social work informed with the Christian sense of involvement and personalism is the highest form of assistance which the Church can render on a human level. The danger in objectivity is impersonality, and the danger of great skill is the sense of manipulative power it gives the one who is using it. These dangers may be avoided if the worker approaches his task with a deep sense of humility, based on the knowledge that Christ dwells in the person whom he serves. This attitude gives a passionate concern and warmth to the worker and makes the entire process a healing one.

A Christian worker, for example, has referred to her an unmarried mother who is being sought by the State Board of Child Welfare. The mother is panicky; she fears arrest and fears that the child will be taken away. Society and tax considerations call for her being subjected to both these things. A secular worker's task would be fulfilled if she accomplished them, for it could be argued that her client in this case is the baby, who should be taken away from the mother, and that the community should be protected from another such act. The Christian worker, however, has a further obligation. Whatever the outcome and disposition of the case, she should minister to the mother, allaying her fear, dealing with her guilt, giving her courage to once again face life. In other words, the worker should treat her as a person, restoring her as much as possible to human dignity and becoming so emotionally involved with her as to be flexible in the enforcement of the necessary regulation. The young mother thus would be healed by the loving concern of the worker, freed from her fear, and enabled, perhaps, to turn to God.

The Christian ethos, in cases like this, softens the social work technique. To put it in another light, social work is aimed at making the client an independent human being who no longer needs to lean on the agency; this is good for the agency as well as for the client. The clergyman, however, often tends to encourage a flattering dependency upon himself or a neurotic dependency on the Church. If he had the psychiatric insight of the caseworker, he could spot a neurotic religious tendency and help the person grow out of it, even if this meant that person was not eternally hanging around the church. Thus do pastoral and social work insights complement each other.

THE CHURCH AGENCY

The marriage of social work and the Church in a church agency, if executed properly, can be a glorious thing; each can be a complement to the other. To put it more accurately, the Church is never more pastorally effective than when her members are using a combination of social work technique and Christian love. At one time I was privileged to work closely with the Youth Consultation Service of the Diocese of Newark in Jersey City. A great deal of learning resulted. Our social worker found that the tightly scheduled interview calendar became chaotic, that the difference between an interview and a walk to the station with a youngster was immaterial, and that group therapy and talking to a bunch of kids through a window were not so far apart. We clergy learned to make referrals through a supervisor, not directly, for the supervisor is responsible for the worker's load. We learned that a case was not casually dropped because a person missed an appointment. We learned to look for other reasons than the one the client gave when he came to see us. For instance, a child would profess interest in going away to school. We didn't run for the school catalogues. The child, if we were patient, would get around to telling us that her father was drunk the night before and that she really wanted *him* to go away. With patience and understanding, the social worker can learn flexibility and over-all concern and the clergyman can learn the advantages of disciplined alertness. There are many other aspects of this mutual education; it has its difficulties as a relationship but the overcoming of them is well worth the effort.

The church agency, however, can use the Church in a wrong way, looking to her merely as a means of support. The rest of the Church also can use the agency in a wrong way. If a drunk calls in the middle of the night, a lazy rector can call the agency! This is hardly a proper referral! The intake policy of a church agency

Furthermore, the diocese, district, or presbytery with a good agency has within it a means of training its clergy; this factor is, unfortunately, neglected. I know how much I learned as a completely green priest from the Youth Consultation Service in Newark. I learned because of fortunate chance, but it would seem that without much effort a good orientation course could be given to the younger clergy which would save them many painful and embarrassing experiences. Likewise, the new workers in the agency could use a few hours of indoctrination by an experienced parish priest. Most of the misunderstanding and friction that occurs between the professions is due to ignorance.

Let us take as an example of this misunderstanding the business of referral. Do the clergy know what the agency can do and what it *cannot* do? Is there agreement on who is in the driver's seat after the referral is made? (Two counselors cannot be in charge at the same time; one must be in a purely supportive role.) The need for constant communication has to be acknowledged, so that both the pastor and caseworker know what the other is doing.

All of this discussion is based upon the hypothesis that a church social agency is vitally necessary in every urban diocese, district, or presbytery. It should be a part of the healing instrumentality of the Church, a place of specialization for those problems which cannot be handled effectively by a clergyman, and a place of experimentation in the art of modern pastoral theology where the warmth and power of the love of God pervades the professional work of highly skilled technicians.

A vital point is that the church agency must be absolutely topflight in its professional standards. We cannot afford amateurish well-meaning sentimentality. This can be as disastrous as having an amateurish well-meaning doctor working in a church hospital. The agency's standards and salary scale must be on a par with those of the best secular agencies in the community.

Finally, the presence of a church agency in a community has a high witness value. It is a spelling-out of the fact that the Church is concerned with the entire community as well as with its own members. For it has always been the policy of the Episcopal Church, for example, to serve people whether they happen to belong to the Church or not. Of course, it often follows that these people find our Lord and the Church through the loving concern experienced by them during crises in their lives.

I would like to share with you a dream of the ideal church agency. It would be centrally located and organized on a diocesan or district level. Its staff would be highly trained and more competent than the staff of any other community agency. A worker would be assigned to every three or four churches, depending upon the need, and would see clients in the offices of the parish to which they belonged. He thus could identify with the local community and learn its resources. There would be a separate supervisor for every three or four workers; he also would conduct a continuous educational program in human relations for clergy, Church School teachers, and volunteer workers and coordinate the entire program on a local level. The central staff would be large enough to back up and support the workers in the field in whatever way possible. There would be a business manager to relieve the director of financial worries, so that he could spend time in education on a diocesan level and in whatever research and study would be necessary to keep the agency alive and vital. The agency would serve all persons with problems and provide group workers where this was expedient. If this dream ever became a reality, I think the Church would wonder how she ever did without it.

THE ROLE OF THE PARISH CHURCH

Many will come to a church for help who have a prejudice against social work or no knowledge of its resources. The Church plays a valuable role here in intelligent referral either to a church or a secular agency. Once the casework process has begun, there is often need for interpretation; misunderstanding between the client and the social worker can easily arise. At this point, a pastor who understands what the worker is trying to accomplish can re-establish the client's confidence and smooth over what otherwise might have been a serious break in their relationship. After the social work agency has done its job, the parish community can be a welcoming place in which the client can once more lead a normal life. There is often a stigma attached to the kind of problem which brings a person to a social agency— broken family, unmarried mother, delinquency, or poverty. Acceptance on the part of some warm community of persons may be essential to the completion of the healing process.

There is another way in which the Church can help. Social workers themselves often live under considerable pressure; often they cannot share this pressure with their supervisors. Thus there is an important ministry *to* the social worker which can be rendered by an understanding clergyman or layman. The profession is still downgraded in many cities; from time to time newspapers or politicians campaign against the alleged abuses of particular public agencies. Here is a point where the Church can reassure the social worker of the high importance of his calling and, in some cases, protect him from abuse by making a well-chosen public statement.

THE PARISH AND
LAW-ENFORCEMENT AGENCIES

The relationship of the Church and law-enforcement agencies poses some special problems. One night in a certain city the phone rang. "Is this Father Moore?" the caller asked. "We got Kolack down here tonight, and we're warning you not to come down. We got him red-handed this time, and we're giving him the business." Here is a case of a complete breakdown of communication. The precinct that was calling was known familiarly as the "Bloody First" among the people of the neighborhood. The police had long protected themselves by the strong-arm and fear method, and the result was an abiding hatred toward them in the neighborhood. Whenever someone presumed to question this method he was told to mind his own business. Our purpose in always coming to the police station when one of our people was arrested was to interpret the due process of law to the arrested person and to use our rapport as a mediating factor with the police so that they would have cooperation from the arrested person. Contrariwise, we were there to protect our parishioner from injustice and police brutality. Our over-all aim was to help the police to become a respected force in the community, rather than an object of fear and hatred. We saw ourselves as allies, but often the police saw us as enemies at worst and at best as a hindrance to the quick execution of slipshod justice with the rubber hose.

Another example may be cited: A priest is sitting in on a juvenile court case concerning an unmarried girl who is in her second pregnancy at the age of sixteen. The case is heard in all of its complications. The judge says to the girl, "Don't you know what you did was wrong?"

"Yessir."

"Don't you know that you let down your minister?"

"Yessir."

"Have you been to Church lately?"

"No sir."

"Well, I'm going to put you in the care of the Reverend Mr. Smith here, and I want you to promise to do what he says and to go to Church. Case dismissed."

Here again communication has broken down. The judge either

has a magical faith in the power of the round collar or he is taking the easy way out of a messy situation. The clergyman has come to the court *not* to procure the girl's release, but merely to be there with her during her trouble and to be of help in providing background information.

There are other instances where there has been a breakdown of communication and the Church has been more of a hindrance than a help. Frankly, when I started my ministry I made many errors in judgment, and I still do. The solution is not anger, but mutual education and understanding. We must rid ourselves of stereotypes like "flatfoot" and "dumb cop" on the one hand and "do-gooder," "sucker," or "starry-eyed idealist" on the other.

From even such a sketchy background, one definite recommendation may be made: the clergy should establish communication on a local level with the police, probation and parole officials, and court officials. Depending on the size of the city, this could be done on an entire city or a particular neighborhood basis. A half-day conference would be a possible way to begin; one or two resource people who have had experience in the field of cooperation might be included. This would be mostly an opportunity to get to know and understand one another and to see the problems of the community through each other's eyes. If this were done at least once a year, informal relationships of trust could be established as a basis for day-to-day cooperation. The results might be amazing. Many clergy hesitate to become involved in this area of work because they are afraid they would be interfering. With a little encouragement they would learn otherwise. One might even wish to include a few social workers at such meetings, so that a sense of teamwork could be established for a given neighborhood.

One of the most difficult areas of relationship grows out of the role of the Church as prophet and pastor, as critic of injustice as well as cooperator in law enforcement and the prevention of crime. The Church has a vocation to speak out against injustice. However, it is at this very point that one comes up against the power structure of the community. For example, fighting against police brutality may destroy the very rapport which is so important for cooperative work in the community.

Finally, a few words about the field of rehabilitation are in order. A parolee is faced with tremendous emotional and psychological problems, as well as economic and social ones. The clergyman can deal more effectively than anyone in this field by being a warm, strengthening, and trusting friend when the parolee feels like an outcast and has little confidence in himself. Someone must be there to accept him and to listen to his long dark fears. This side of his rehabilitation is even more important than his finding a job, because on his sense of self-confidence often hangs his chance for a job. Furthermore, the clergyman can interpret to him the program of the parole officer, whom the parolee may not trust at first. The parish family also can be an accepting community within which a new life can be built.

The clergyman is the only person with whom the delinquent is involved who does not change. The delinquent is arrested by a policeman, supervised by a jailer, investigated by a pretrial investigator, advised by a lawyer, accused by a prosecutor, and sentenced by a judge. Perhaps he is referred to a probation officer, or he is sentenced to prison where he is again related to wardens, social workers, psychologists, psychiatrists, attendants, and teachers. Upon his release, he is put in the custody of a parole officer, whose load is usually so heavy that he hardly knows the delinquent. There is little wonder none of these relationships has much chance of being "therapeutic." On the other hand, the clergyman continues his relationship before, during, and after the whole process, even visiting the prison when feasible. Thus, he can be a steadying influence and an interpreter of the rather complicated processes and aims of the various other people involved. He can absorb hostility and complement the other relationships. (These comments would apply to patients committed to mental hospitals as well.)

All of this work takes infinite patience; it is full of failure and disappointment, and it requires skill and tact. Those with whom we work will probably seldom become productive members of the Church in the usual sense. Nevertheless, when we serve those in need and those in prison, we serve the Lord himself, and we must give him the best we have.

13. The Parish and Social Action

"Politics are, or should be, part of caritas; they are the matter to which the form of caritas must be applied."

—CHARLES WILLIAMS

SOCIAL action is as necessary as a Sunday School to the life of a parish. It is so integral to an effective urban parish that we have already mentioned it frequently, but because of its importance, controversiality, and complexity, we may well consider the subject further. Social action is an essential part of the ministry of the Body of Christ. Let us be clear about the reasons.

1. Jesus came to redeem the world—not the individual alone, but all of society. Therefore, the Church must be effective in the redemption of the social structure.

2. Unless the Church is involved in society, unless it expresses incarnate, sacramental concern, it does not look like Jesus, is not evangelical, and in fact may keep people away from our Lord. Many persons who have never been remotely interested suddenly catch fire when the Church begins to look like the Church. On the other hand, others who have perhaps been coming for narrow reasons may be driven away (as was the rich young ruler).

3. Charity cannot be expressed toward an individual who is being crushed by such social forces as bad housing, unemployment, or discrimination, without an attempt to alleviate those conditions. If the Church does not seek to do all in its power to help such a person, it is not being charitable.

4. Social action grows out of the Eucharist, especially the theology of the Offertory, where all of life is offered to God. As the individual must confess his sins and purpose amendment as part of his offering, so the Church in making her social offerings must be attempting social amendment.

5. All the world is the creation of the Father. He and his Church are therefore concerned with all the world.

Having stressed involvement, one must also stress caution, for unwise social action can do more harm than good in our ideologically sensitive age. Many Christians who are persons of integrity sincerely differ over the method whereby certain agreed-upon social goals should be reached. They differ over the timing of the social change, the type of involvement of the Church as institution, and the priority of sometimes conflicting values such as economic freedom and security. We should not "go easy," but we must be quite clear in rationale, method, and objective.

In addition to a general theological rationale, a "local" rationale is necessary. Social action makes the most sense to its participants and to the general public—hence is most effective—when it is closely tied to the concern of the parish or locality. For instance, to clean up a vacant lot next door to the parish house for use as a playground and to press the city to provide equipment for it is clearly a proper Christian concern of immediately observable value. One step further removed, and hence a little more difficult and controversial, would be a program of providing legal assistance to tenants against unfair rent. Here one is in jeopardy, as is the person for whom the program is being carried out, because if it fails, the tenant may be evicted.

A further-removed step would be a program protesting police brutality. Here even more criticism may be forthcoming, and those involved are even more liable to retribution. Finally, a full-scale battle with City Hall involving other agencies and groups (the benefits of which campaign may seem to critics very indirect) is even harder to justify and participants are even harder to enroll. The goal is more distant and less distinct, the techniques are more complicated, and the danger of retaliation is even more evident.

Each effort enumerated above is definitely a legitimate social action program; yet the last is more difficult than the first. It is less immediate and more complicated in technique, involves a wider range of participating entities, and takes longer.

DEVELOPING A PROGRAM

The beginning of any social action program in a parish should be on as simple a base as possible—where results are rather quick and easily seen. Then, as the parish or committee grows in confidence, it can proceed to the more difficult projects. In this way, the action grows out of the immediate need of the parish (a playground) or of its parishioners (rent control). As the social action group becomes more knowledgeable and sophisticated it can adopt a goal more for the general good. But proceeding from the specific, immediate, partially selfishly motivated project develops confidence and know-how needed to carry on the less immediate, more unselfish program. Nothing discourages a group more than initial failure. Thus, the first project might well be sponsored by the parish alone because working with other groups has its own complications.

The beginnings of a program are quite simple in an inner-city situation. As soon as the parish has a few families from the neighborhood involved in its life, the clergyman will quickly learn what their immediate problems are. He can then call a meeting either at the church or in someone's home or apartment to which all concerned within and without the parish are invited. At this meeting, through discussion, an objective can be ascertained and temporary leadership assigned. If possible, the clergyman should *not* be chairman, even though he may have the best qualifications.

A second meeting could plan strategy and timing and assign jobs. It might be that the project can function best as a neighborhood group with no official connection with the church, or perhaps it would be to the ultimate benefit of both the church and the project to have it sponsored by a church group. The primary goal is to get the job done; the secondary goal is to show the church's identification with the project for purposes of evangelism. It is always helpful to have a lawyer available for advice, for almost any project has legal angles.

The clergyman must be patient and bear with the inefficiency which is built into the inner-city situation. He should continue to remind, advise, exhort, or recruit, but the actual leadership belongs in the hands of laymen wherever this is possible. When the objective has been reached, one should not insist on keeping the committee alive unless it still has vitality. It is often better to let a committee die and call together another for the next project.

It may be that the job is too big for the parish. In this case, the church can be the catalyst for forming an alliance with other "nonpolitical" socially concerned groups such as labor unions, the NAACP, the Urban League, Elks, Masons (especially Negro branches), and other churches. This kind of intergroup council has its advantages and disadvantages. It should be loosely structured so that full permission of all groups is not necessary for each project; if such unanimous agreement were required, the job might never be done. When the executive committee organizes a project, each constituent organization should be notified; if any group does not wish to be included, it can so state. Meanwhile, however, each group remains in general sympathy with the over-all purpose, and each name appears on the stationery of the inter-group committee.

Another way to structure such a council is through individual rather than organizational membership. Such a group relies on the individuals to form *ad hoc* task forces of their own organizations for each specific project. In this case, the executive committee acts as a watchdog or quarterback and calls upon the necessary individuals or groups for the job at hand. It coordinates subcommittees which concern themselves with specific projects, such as housing, law enforcement, or employment, and rallies the whole organization when its strength is needed.

There are other goals which call for an even higher level of power; some ends may only be secured by enacting new state laws. In this case, the appropriate denominational department should be asked to assist and to organize the strengths of the proper groups on a city or state level.

One must be careful not to become involved in partisan politics as the concern grows from a neighborhood to a city-wide effort. The Church as an institution backs *issues* rather than parties or men. Only rarely, and with great care, can the Church tie herself to a candidate or party; for when she does, she is involved in the compromises of candidates or party. On the other hand, the *individual* Christian must be a political man and be as careful a steward of his vote as he is of his dollar. A notable exception to this rule of keeping the Church per se out of partisan politics in unorganized, highly corrupt situations was a situation in East Harlem.[1]

The rather difficult areas are those in which the Church must

[1] Bruce Kenrick, *Come Out the Wilderness* (New York: Harper & Row, 1962), pp. 209 ff.

ally herself with other organizations in order to accomplish an end. Here we must not be too pure. Let us say there is violation of the minimum wage law in a given city, and this directly affects the members of the Church. Is there any reason the Church should not ally herself with labor unions to redress this wrong? Or, if racial discrimination exists in a local restaurant, why should the Church not ally with the NAACP?

There is often an inverse relationship between the level of respectability of any given social action group and the vigor of its performance. One is often faced with a choice of organizing the power structure which has the power but not the will, or organizing those affected by injustice who have the will but not the power. Experience has shown that the latter is more effective. In a democracy even the powerless have access to power, as has been shown by the sit-down strikes of the thirties or the sit-ins of the sixties. The Christian must believe in the power of the technique of nonviolence.

The Reverend James A. Gusweller accomplished more, almost singlehanded, in New York City than did the church-going presidents of the real estate organizations or the city administration. The same can be said even more strongly about the Reverend Martin Luther King and many others. The little inner-city parish should not be discouraged because none of those in the power structure is in attendance; this may be a blessing and may free the parish to be more vigorous than its more powerful neighbors.

The only requisites for a start are three dedicated, stubborn people and a little know-how. The latter is obtainable from the nearest Urban League, NAACP, labor union, ACLU chapter, or community organizer. It is unnecessary to copy them, but usually within their ranks one will find men with knowledge of social action techniques.

Accompanying publicity is a great help, if used wisely; examples of this are photographs of dirty lots or hazardous housing, and sermons typed up in press-release style. Advice in these techniques may be obtained from local churchmen in the newspaper profession.

SOME PROGRAMS COMPLETED

Perhaps some of these principles will be clarified in the following case histories. They illustrate what can actually be accomplished by Christians who are convinced of the necessity of the Church's participation in social action programs.

VACANT LOTS FOR TINY TOTS

A parish noticed the need for more play space in the inner city. A committee met, and vacant lots were chosen. Newspapers were notified of the neighborhood cleanup. When the news photographer was about to take a picture, the City Sanitation Department representatives arrived. The city took credit for the idea of the cleanup and in exchange offered some play equipment. Objectives were broadened, and other neighborhoods were involved. A motorcade including a float with play equipment was organized. A catchy slogan was chosen—"Vacant Lots, for Tiny Tots." Children with pence cans collected money for play equipment, and a benefit field-day bazaar raised money for the same purpose. The results were that four or five vacant lots became more interesting play areas; a good deal of newspaper and neighborhood publicity showed the Church's concern; church and nonchurch people were involved in a valid, if simple, community project, with the cooperation of City Hall.

RENT CONTROL CLINICS

The existence of a law on the books is no guarantee of protection. Frequently it is necessary to inform people that they are protected by the law and to help them to seek that protection. In the early 1950's the rent control of tenements in an eastern city allowed a 20 per cent increase under certain conditions. This was the occasion for much maneuvering on the part of slum landlords. The people were ignorant of their rights. A clergyman called a meeting of all the families in an affected tenement and informed them that they need not pay the projected rent increase; they agreed to stand together in this matter, since presumably the landlord could not evict them all. When the rent fell due, however, they all paid the illegal increase since they were fearful of eviction and, with some justification, did not trust the judgment of the clergyman whom some had just met for the first time. It took several more meetings and mutual encouragement to stiffen resistance.

From this experience, it became clear that there was a need for rent control clinics in which each neighborhood would have accurate information available and through which morale and the will to resist could be enhanced. At the peak of this effort, five such clinics were meeting regularly in the apartments of parishioners or their friends, and through their efforts many families were saved from paying illegally high rent. Obviously, legal counsel was sought throughout all the proceedings, which included an occasional lawsuit against a landlord. Unfortunately, one family was evicted, and the case was lost; this illustrates the risk involved in such ventures.

PUBLIC HOUSING INTEGRATION

High rents were not the only difficulty. Housing was simply not available for some at *any* rental figure. One family, living in a coal bin, was finally evicted by the Welfare Department, but no housing could be found for almost a year. In the meantime, the children lived in the rectory and the hospital.

Thus the parish was faced with breaking the pattern of discrimination in the low-cost public housing. For this purpose, an intergroup council was formed; it included about twenty non-political organizations. The executive committee, including a clergyman, a Negro lawyer from the parish, a Jewish lawyer, and several others, took the issue to City Hall, to the senator in Washington by letter, and to the local Federal Housing office. Finally, after a long and baffling series of events, broken promises, insults, and frustrations, the heretofore white housing projects were desegregated. Even the heretofore Negro project included some white families in a token effort.

POLICE PROTECTION IN PUBLIC HOUSING PROJECTS

Many city parishioners live in such "projects." In the summer, when the weather is hot, tempers are short, and boys have little to do; the gangs are abroad, and tension mounts. One evening a priest, calling in a project, found himself in the center of a serious situation. The project police were untrained; one of them panicked and shot off a pistol. Without the intervention of the priest, an extremely bloody race riot might have occurred. The social action attempted in response to this incident was to draw up a petition requesting that trained police be assigned to the projects. An amusing sidelight in the campaign was that three summer-staff college students on their first day of work with the parish were arrested for circulating the petition by the very police against whom it was directed. The students were asked their legal residence, and it appeared all were from out of town and one was from England. Immediately, they were thought to be communists—something of a compliment for Episcopalians, under the circumstances.

A HUMAN RELATIONS COUNCIL

In a certain small metropolis the organized human relations organizations had been polarized between the so-called "Uncle

Tom" paternalistic approach and a rather more radical approach. No third force was available to speak to the rapidly changing times. An Episcopal priest cooperated with a Roman monseignor, a Jewish rabbi, a Negro staff member of a respectable settlement house, and a handful of dedicated and hard-working Unitarians and agnostics to found a Human Relations Council. The primary purpose was to lobby for an effective Mayor's Commission on Human Rights. When this goal was accomplished, the group remained in existence as a quiet, behind-the-scenes force for better "human relations." It is well to note that an official commission always needs an unofficial group to keep it alive and strong.

RACE RELATIONS:
THE CHRISTIAN VIEW

Before this chapter on social action is concluded, a special word must be said about race relations, even though the subject is far too vast to be adequately covered here. In one aspect or another, this is the primary problem of the inner-city residential area. More and more, in the cities of America, the inner city and the ghetto are coterminous, and any clergyman or lay leader in the inner city should be knowledgeable in this field. The myths and stereotypes about minority groups are persistent and difficult to stamp out; the psychological and sociological problems of race relations are exceedingly complex. A few principles about the Church's vocation in this area may well be outlined here.

The Church must be absolutely loud and clear concerning her unalterable stand against discrimination within her own life. This does not mean that every individual communicant or even every parish group will become integrationist overnight. It does mean that in word and action the leadership of the Church must be unequivocal.

We must understand the peculiar vocation of the Church in

this regard. First, she must witness to the clarity of God's word on the principle of the equality of every man's worth in the eyes of God. Second, she must be a patient teacher of this principle as it articulates itself in existential situations in the community. Third, she is called to be a center of action, appropriate to the kind of parish, for racial justice. Finally, the Church, as reconciler, must exercise the power of Christian love in the fearless exchange of ideas within the trust of the Christian family, in the breaking down of age-old defenses and barriers, in the exposing and healing of deep wounds, and in the partnership of corporate action. The Church can be one of the few places where people, separated in all other areas of life, can come together and talk.

Let no one underestimate the difficulty of the task. In *Christians in Racial Crisis,* a study of Little Rock, Thomas F. Pettigrew and Ernest Q. Campbell show clearly that the more closely identified a pastor becomes with his congregation, the less likely is he to take a stand (the newest pastors in Little Rock were the boldest). It is also pointed out that the more powerful the Church is in the community social structure, the less likely is its pastor to bear witness. This gives evidence to a sad irony—that the two qualities which could make a witness most effective, the rapport of a man with his congregation and the congregation's influence in the community, both seem to militate against courageous action.

The Church has the clearest rationale on which to base an ideology of human relations. Christianity values the dignity of the individual, whosoever he may be, and spells forth equality of worth in the eyes of God without sentimentalizing or overcompensating ideas of intellectual or social equality which may or may not exist. Christian love has to do with mind, will, and concern rather than with inappropriate emotion, whether positive or negative. Furthermore, since prejudice *is* an emotional and irrational thing, the Church can use the appropriate emotion of Christian love as a force more effective than pure reason alone.

For all those who leave the parish or the Church for reasons of racial prejudice, there will be others who are drawn to it because of its courage. As the years go by and times change, the number who seek the Church for the right reasons should grow. We are not heading for easier, less earnest times.

As the program to equalize civil rights changes rapidly toward direct action and demonstration, every Christian should be ready to carry a sign and, as the Rt. Rev. Daniel Corrigan says, "offer his body" to the cause of racial justice.

14. The Clergyman's Family in the Inner City

BY MRS. PAUL MOORE

"A certain brother said, 'It is right for a man to take up the burden for them who are near him, whatever it may be, and so to speak to put his own soul in the place of that of his neighbor, and to become, if it were possible, a double man, and he must suffer, and weep, and mourn with him, and finally the matter must be accounted by him as if he himself had acquired his countenance and soul, and he must suffer for him as he would for himself. For thus it is written, we are all one body, and this passage also informs us concerning the holy and mysterious kiss.'"

—CHARLES WILLIAMS

ON Jersey Avenue, across from a shiny new supermarket, two white brick houses have recently been built. They stand within a block of Grace Church and are the first private dwellings to be built in this area of Jersey City in fifty years. They are obviously not evidences of some grand urban renewal project, for they overlook dirty gutters and deteriorating sidewalks and adjoin a closed-down funeral parlor, that depressing symbol of a neighborhood on the skids. They are, instead, a gamble on the part of a fuzzy-headed or far-sighted realtor. Some would consider the building of these two houses a significant and encouraging step. Time will tell.

When we moved to Jersey City in August of 1949 with a three-year-old girl, a two-year-old boy, and a new baby soon to arrive, there were no signs of a future. A dilapidated brownstone house with ironwork betraying its earlier fashion occupied the site of the supermarket. Real estate men were not contemplating anything creative. The lifting of rent controls in 1949 had encouraged realtors to convert brownstone singles and doubles into rooming houses with exorbitant rents. The downswing was still underway.

Our moving van rumbled through the Holland tunnel from West 21 Street, New York City, where we spent our seminary years to 2nd Street, Jersey City, on a hot, muggy day. The rectory, with a Charles Addams' slant to its brownstone facade, was set back some thirty feet from the sidewalk and its front walk adjoined the street by a lich gate. Over the gate, in manuscript letters, were carved the words, "Enter His gates with thanksgiving," and attached to the connecting fence was a handpainted sign: "Keep Out." At this time, because of this admonition, there was a plot of green grass forming a possible play yard of about twenty feet square, but the only trace of life when we arrived was a dying dog. Our first acts, accomplished with nervous zeal, were to summon the S.P.C.A. and rip off the offending sign. Then we tried to bring some order to the house.

For at least twenty years the rectory had been occupied by childless couples: most recently, a Church Army officer and his wife and before that by a Canon who was an intimate of the famous Mayor Hague. There were those who said it was the Canon's ghost who rambled around the house with a noisy set of keys. Very few of the nine rooms had served as much more than storerooms, and the first week was spent literally filling Sal-

vation Army trucks with hundreds of church magazines and
quantities of broken-down furnishings and hospital equipment.
The dirt was the dirt of years and of disuse; much of it remained
after our efforts. The cleaning kept us busy those first days when
we met no one. The three black-suited men (my husband and
our two bachelor colleagues, and I, a pregnant companion,
were eyed very strangely when we walked the streets. The first
Sunday morning was a dismal one with a congregation of twenty-
five in a church built to seat eight hundred.

Within ten days of moving in, we were joined by our two children. They had been staying with their grandmother about
thirty miles away in the country while we went through the
process of what we quaintly called getting settled.

Physically, the house had great potential charm; there were
high ceilings, large windows, electrified gas fixtures (one leaked
and caused momentary alarm), and parquet floors somewhat the
worse for wear. This charm was combined with such uncomfortable features as two narrow closets for the entire house, a
kitchen sink appropriate for someone four feet tall, a hopeless
hot water system, and a highly temperamental furnace. These
annoyances are surmountable and even fun when you and your
children are young and the standards of the affluent society have
not grasped you as tightly as they have me in the ensuing years.
No doubt the situation could have been improved had more in-
genious people been involved.

The two unmarried clergy occupied the third floor; the Moores,
growing to a family of six children before we left in 1957, took
over the second floor with its three bedrooms and one bath. The
downstairs consisted of a connecting living room and dining
room, which was used for a multiplicity of purposes including
office space (until another building was acquired in 1953), and
a kitchen that was for eating, passing the time of day, and above
all, talking.

AN OPEN RECTORY

It was into this kitchen that people came at almost any time of the day or night. It was here that the invisible reality of the action of the altar became for many a visible reality. It was here that George Grace, a Bowery "bum," asked for a match and said, "I really am the beggar but I feel at home." It was here that Diana, three months' pregnant from an encounter in a tenement doorway, told me she was scared of what would happen on her wedding night. It was here that Jim, an unskilled laborer, when sympathy was offered for his dying wife, said, "But it is such a loving time." Seated at the kitchen table, a moneyless Negro, when asked why he would borrow for an expensive funeral for his wife, explained, "We don't do too well in this world so we've got to have a big send-off." And it was in this place that a seminarian, now a seasoned priest, said, "I'd like to stay in this kitchen forever." I must say I cannot go quite as far as that remark! The kitchen and its company were not unique, but there existed a reality which is not everyday fare for most of us— conversation between people from every conceivable race, creed, color, and background in an intimate milieu. There was further reality in the conversation of those whose major concern is survival in terms of food and shelter and whose philosophy of life leaves very little gap between expectation of what life might bring and what life is. A current author has called this "a realistic adaptation to a socially perverse situation."

We chose to operate the house on an open-door principle, although this became less true as our own children grew older and more numerous. I do not think this is imperative in every situation. For us, it began that way. The church was next door, and there was no office space; therefore, this was where people came.

The majority of the parish lived in substandard housing with

unspeakable plumbing and inadequate heat; television and parties were their only respite at home. Even our simple house
represented a haven for those who visited it. This existence made
the Christian faith come alive for me, and our children did not
know any other church life existed. The old saw—"In Christ
there is no color-line"—made sense; feeding the hungry and
sheltering the homeless were commonplace. Mrs. Welles had
been living in a whitewashed coal bin with eleven children;
some of them stayed with us while we found a house for them.
There were the Bowery men who came to the door for soup or
coffee. Often this life was difficult; often the people were offen-
sive. We were rarely noble, but we were often shaken. It is
shocking for the Christian to hear Christianity criticized, and
it is shocking to practice it. Nevertheless, the crucifixion was on
our doorstep.

As time went on, the children and teen-age groups in the
church became predominantly Negro while the adult group
remained about 40 per cent white. The church's immediate neighborhood, running a block in each direction, was white and almost
entirely Roman Catholic. However, our relations with the Roman
clergy and some of our neighbors were not so much hostile as
non-existent. The first autumn, our tiny congregation was standing on the sidewalk after the eleven o'clock service. The Holy
Name Society, complete with the Mayor, countless Monsignors,
others in holiday mood, and a parochial school band, was ap-
proaching in its annual parade. After a whispered and lengthy
consultation of those in command, the clergy's top hats were
tipped in our direction. I can still see those hats glistening in
the noon sunshine.

Other relationships were more articulate. An elderly man with
a loud voice and an Italian accent called us a "bunch o' phonies."
A petition, signed by some of the residents in the block, was sent

to our bishop requesting that the church which used to be so peaceful and well-behaved resume its quiet ways.

CHILDREN IN THE RECTORY

Our own children had a good life. They had friends in the two tenement houses adjoining the rectory, although our neighbors were for the most part adults. They played with the children from the church and our block in the concrete yard which had soon replaced the green grass in front of the rectory. Ours was the only yard on that street, so the activities of the younger children were always in full view. Our daughters had friends whom they enjoyed, and their companions never showed any behavior problems that would not be found in other neighborhoods. The teen-age gang troubles that existed were never in any way connected with hostility or violence towards younger children. Our oldest boy, who lived in Jersey City until he was ten, formed a very close friendship with a Negro boy that continued long after we moved away. There was identification of the other variety when our two-year-old reported in a loud shriek, "Some goddam nigger took my shovel."

The most difficult picture to give is that of education, partly because one should be able to be more precise than I will be, and partly because education, like politics, is an area of life about which people feel strongly if they take a stand at all.

There are those who want excellence in teaching and in conditions, including equipment and environment. There are those, among whom I would class myself, who want very much a good score on these educational qualities, but passionately hope to have the school provide other opportunities for learning than the courses of study: in short, that it help teach the child how to live. If you belong to the former group, there are many things that would offend you about P.S. 71 in Jersey City, New Jersey (and I suspect about P.S. ? in many American suburbs), and a young clergyman might make every effort not to send his child there. However, if you share the latter view, you would find many "pluses." This school was no junior blackboard jungle. Because this was in a heavily Roman Catholic area, the public schools were not overcrowded, and our children's teachers were excellent. They were going to school with the same children they played with; we were not removing them part-time from the life we had chosen for them.

We had our eldest child tested at one of the leading New York City private schools after she had completed the second grade, and she had accomplished as much as her Manhattan counterparts in most areas of study and was ahead of them in a few. At the end of her fourth school year we found ourselves concerned about competition and sent her and her younger brother to an Episcopal parochial school in lower New York, one stop on the subway from Jersey City. They were accompanied in the morning by parishioners who worked in that area, and they returned by themselves. We loved the school, although we are not parochial school devotees; the Christian training was at its best, and our debt to St. Luke's and the children's devotion to it are considerable. Whether the change was necessary for adequate preparation through the sixth grade (our eldest was at this level when we moved to Indiana) is debatable. Had it involved more of a commuting problem for the children or had it meant a "fancy" school we would not have taken the step.

Community living and constant traffic were both very demanding, and for this reason we were rigid about what privacy we had as a couple and as a family. My husband and I were able to get away for twenty-four hours at least every two weeks, and return restored; a devoted friend in the Bronx came to care for the children. As for family life, breakfast and lunch were relatively quiet, although there were always interruptions. The hour after supper, provided someone was available to answer the doorbell and telephone, was a time to retreat upstairs for stories and prayers. Again, because we were aware as the years went on that it would be easy not to find time for such things, we made more of an effort to use the time creatively than we would have in other circumstances (or do now!). We had contests to familiarize the children with the Hymnal and the Book of Common Prayer; we had charade evenings, acting out saints' names, Bible passages, and the like (these have remained among the children's favorite hours). We collected books and records that we found helpful and discarded others that were dry and tedious. We tried at different seasons of the Church year to have food associated with liturgical feasts in different parts of the world, drawing the line at a macabre little custom I dug up of having white pudding with raspberry sauce for Holy Innocents!

One of our favorite customs is a German one known as "Christ Kindl" and is sometimes referred to in our house as "that Advent routine of Mommy's." The first Sunday in Advent is marked by a special dinner, with a noticeable improvement in menu, table setting, and apparel—including everyone's presence at the same table at the same meal! The first candle on the Advent wreath is lighted by the youngest child, the Collect and Gospel for that Sunday are read by other children, and finally a bowl is passed around. In the bowl are slips of paper, each bearing the name of a different member of the family above the age of five (with some misgivings, this has resolved itself as the age of reason). Each person is to draw the name of another. Obviously, there are recurrent crises: you draw the same name you had last year, your own name, or that of someone with whom you have been fighting all week. After numerous dry runs, the dinner is over and the four weeks of Advent have begun. From this day until Christmas, you do something each day for the person whose name you have drawn, and he becomes for you this Advent the Christ Child in the manger while you, remaining anonymous in the little efforts at love and generosity, partake of the Christ-like spirit. With all its imperfections, as the days go on the custom takes on real meaning.

One word of warning about family prayers, customs, traditions and the like is in order. I am convinced that the old truism that "what works for one does not necessarily work for the other" was never more applicable than in this area. None of my descriptions should be thought of as techniques. Traditions some families might find unbearably stuffy, others would enjoy; activities some would find self-conscious or too "cute," would appeal to others. The point is that an offering of some kind is made.

"THESE THINGS WE SHARED"

There is an old Irish law which reads, "You shall never shut the light from another man's window." I used to be teased about this because I quoted it at every opportunity and ranted that the slums where our people lived broke this law without exception. Caryll Houselander says that the non-Christian works to alleviate suffering but that the Christian must also share in it. I shared in it only in that with my children, I visited people, and they became our friends. They talked with me of the endless broken-down toilets that froze in winter, of the rats that attacked their children, of the uncollected garbage that littered the yards and alleys, and the inevitable urine stench in the halls and stairways. We would sit in the kitchen or the windowless center room of a railroad flat, and although there were constant reminders that there were barriers between us, we had children and the same neighborhood in common.

Most of the everyday activity in the rectory offends all modern techniques: the unstructured conversations, the giving of food and secondhand clothing at the door with little thought to what use might be made of them ("Won't he sell the overcoat for some wine?"), the extra guests for supper, the general permissive atmosphere. The Cure d'Ars wrote that we are responsible for the giving of alms; we are not responsible for what is done with them. And Gandhi declared, "For the millions who go without two meals a day, the only form in which God dare appear is food."

I have neglected to mention the funny things which happened every day. There was the time an old friend returned for a visit and commented that things had become stuffy and subdued in the rectory. As she spoke, the window opened and an unknown Puerto Rican climbed in, ran through the living room where we sat, and departed silently through another open window. There was Harry, who came to the door for something to eat the first year we were there, got a furnished room a block away, and never left. He had been ill and had stayed behind in Jersey City when the traveling circus left town. He had many stock speeches —one which boomed elephant manure as fertilizer for the tiny churchyard, and he knew he could get us some—and a long yarn about his friendship with Trigger, Roy Rogers' horse, who would "whinner" when he heard Harry's voice. At sixty-five, he had the cocky saunter and vulnerable ego of a six-year-old boy and would race home for his pawnshop pistols and dress Marine blues when one of the children had a new toy. When I would ask him to do one more errand he would mutter, "Mommy, someone's gotta break your miserable spirit." He was very loving and part of the community.

It is hard to end the story; in fact, it continues. The block that was white in 1949 is now almost entirely Negro; money is now being raised for a new parish house to replace the derelict hall we used for gatherings and basketball games; there are new houses and the new supermarket I mentioned. What do these things mean?

Leaving was unbelievably painful and confusing. We did not realize that to even the most sophisticated of the parishioners and to ourselves it would seem to be a betrayal, because we had shared so much. The Sunday the announcement of our departure was to be made, a parishioner and close friend, the only professional man in the congregation, came to the door of the rectory. My husband had told him in confidence that we, for many reasons, had felt we should move on. We shook hands and I remember saying, "Bill, I know you understand." He answered, "I guess you don't really like us." How can you think of this life as just a "specialized ministry" when you leave part of yourself there?

15. *The Future*

"*The sacred City could not be built by everyone raising his own little pile of bricks. Men were to be part of it, and so only it of them. The Eucharist which was the center and consummation of all the Rites, was the union of the City.*"

—CHARLES WILLIAMS

IN THESE chapters, we have wandered around the city and the Church. We have looked over the history and theology of these two organisms; we have analyzed briefly the problems of each and the problem of relating the one to the other. I have taken you into the pulpit and before the altar; you have accompanied me to places of work and rest, to the houses and the churches of the city. We have made suggestions, reported actions, and considered thoughts and principles.

Having done this, having surveyed the present and the past, what prophecy can be seen for the future? The future will be framed by the way the Church deals with the interplay of *continuity* and *change*. This tension between them can be creative or destructive; it can issue forth in new life or paralyzing conflict. Here is an example. There are those in the Church today who would tear down structure because they are shaken—frightened or overelated—by the changes they see, the discrepancy between the changing world, and the stubborn changelessness of the institution of the Church. They would tear down the Church as she exists. Suspect, to them, are her middle-class mores, her segregation; suspect are her denominationalism, her preoccupation with differences in polity and doctrine; suspect is her introversion; suspect are her professionals and their schools, her pomp and circumstance, and her institutionalism.

To them, we would pose these questions. How can the bourgeois mentality be cut out without losing the bourgeois soul which, as St. Therese of Lisieux has shown, can attain sanctity? How can denominationalism be eliminated without losing the knife that cuts and the hook that holds, without spending interminable hours in joint decision and joint planning? How can the clergy be taught about the world and still have time to learn more of the mysteries of the faith? And how can the parish be destroyed before something else is ready to take its place?

Related to this is another question: When Christians are brought together in a nonparochial context (in the context of their working lives, for instance) and their community grows, some organization must come into being and some *place* must be provided for worship, study, and fellowship. Further, this new community will need to have regular communication with other Christian communities. To fulfill these seemingly inevitable needs, something mighty like a parish will come into being, whatever its name may be. In other words, if the parish is eliminated, would not some other organized community, subject to many of the same shortcomings, take its place? Reorganization does not eliminate sin.

Greatest danger of all, in this radical approach, is to spend so much time discussing the need for change that the daily tasks—preaching and teaching, ministry and witness, forgiving and loving, and dying and rising—become forgotten. For whatever stringent steps the Church may take in her reorganization to effect a greater impact upon the structure of society, she is made up of men and women who are members of the Body and upon the depth of whose conversion her power will depend.

This realization forms the basis for the thinking of another school of thought in the Church. Its advocates acknowledge the faults, dangers, and sins enumerated above. They, too, are searching for change and for new ways, but they are not willing to relinquish the parish. For this is where the Christians now gather for the Breaking of the Bread. It is here that God is worshiped still, however badly, however insincerely. There are serious problems in this line of thought, too. Those who stand by the parish while striving to change it are plagued by the sheer weight of the hours spent in sustaining it as now organized. So much time and energy must be given to organization, administration, canvasses, denominational activity, ecumenical encounters, and community cooperation. How much time is left for the leap into the new radical way, even if such a way is discovered, while at the same time maintaining the old conventional way? How does one teach new concepts and old concepts simultaneously? How does one break the old trunk to graft in the new branch?

However, tensions such as this between different approaches, in the very threat they hold for the status quo, are a good thing, for they make local Christians seek justification for their ways. They force questions: Why are we here? Does this parish have a special vocation? Can we fulfill that vocation?

SIGNS OF THE SPIRIT

In this reaching out from the established patterns, several tendencies are appearing. One of these trends, as we have seen, is toward ecumenicity and toward reorganization of the Church into units better equipped to deal with the metropolis. We are barely beginning to overcome parochialism. Our next effort, already upon us, is to overcome "diocesanism." We must learn to carry varied ministries, shared by parishes, sponsored by dioceses or by Church Federations, and sometimes led by laymen. Invisible as well as visible ministries, coordinated and tightly organized as well as relatively uncoordinated and spontaneous ministries, are to be sought up and down the land. This means an openness to the wind of the Spirit, a creative imagination, and a willingness to work with jerry-built structures, especially in the initial phase of a program.

Another trend is the Church's increasing interest in city planning and urban renewal. More and more conferences deal with the Christian's role in the decisions which shape our cities for the years to come. We are painfully learning the techniques of becoming involved in these plans, but there is an intolerable vacuum in what might be called the theology of city planning. The Church wants to have a part in decision, but she has not yet clarified the position she holds. Certain principles exist, to be sure: we ask for decent housing for all—cleanliness, heat, space, plumbing, and fair rent. We stand for open occupancy and integration wherever possible. We continue to insist on adequate recreation facilities and personnel. These goals, for instance, are clear.

However, we also want a sense of community, but we do not know how this can be built into a city neighborhood. We want responsible leadership on the local level, and yet we have backed masses of public housing which by law preclude all but the lowest income groups. (This undercuts leadership and initiative, for those who have the drive to lead are the same, generally, who have the drive to earn an income over the ceiling of such projects. Thus low-cost housing tends to keep together by law the very young and inexperienced families and those families who for one reason or another do not have leadership ability.)

We want a decline in juvenile delinquency and are surprised and shocked that it exists in perhaps a greater degree in the shiny new public housing than in the old slums. We want a city to have spirit and life; yet we unconsciously glorify suburban living which takes blood from the downtown heart of urban greatness. We want a sense of unity in diversity, but are confused by the subtle dynamics of movement whether in terms of residential change or transportation.

The vision of the Kingdom, the Communion of Saints, the Trinity of Persons in the Unity of Love, the doctrine of Man, fallen yet made in the image of God: here is the reservoir of truth from which our theology of city planning can flow. As yet it is not channeled to fit the metropolitan age. But at least the Church is beginning to think on these things.

On a neighborhood level, however, we do slightly better, both in involvement and in solution. In several places the Church has made a definite impact upon its surroundings. At St. Paul's Episcopal Church in New Haven, the parish has been instrumental in the rehabilitation of a whole section of the city around it. In Chicago, through the well-publicized Woodlawn Association, the Presbyterians have been much involved in the decisions which will shape the future of their locality.

Some sections of the metropolis are so specialized in their function that a normal parish cannot begin to serve them. Such an area, the Medical Center in Chicago, is being reached by the flexible ministry of Bishop Anderson House.

Nor have these efforts been confined to limited geographical sections. Numerous Lay Training Centers continue to explore the potentialities of the "ministry of the laity" in an urban society. Small, encouraging experiments come to light: in Houston, for instance, twenty families have put themselves at the disposal of the bishop to be a task force which he can use for any strategic situation he might choose.

With all this and much more going on, the need for communication becomes urgent: communication between parts of the
country, between dioceses, between denominations, and between
the local and national levels of each Church and within the
Council of Churches.

Perhaps the fact that the Church is reaching out in these many
ways is more important than the specific shape of the experimentation, for this vitality is a sure sign of the Spirit and shows
forth a new seriousness in our sense of mission.

Other new ventures are beginning over the country even as
this book is being written. In Chicago, an Interdenominational
Urban Training Center is about to open its doors, supported and
governed by the national bodies of the several denominations
involved. It will offer clinical and academic training in the new
fields of urban life, from summer field work for seminarians to
graduate work for experienced clergy and laymen. In Indianapolis, a three-year research project has begun the task of uncovering the proper ministry for the "Grand Old Parishes" of the
central city to those who work downtown and to those who live
in the high-rise apartments nearby. This effort is under the direction of the Dean of the Cathedral with the advice of a committee
of laymen of varied backgrounds and parishes; it includes the
rectors of the downtown parishes of two neighboring cities.

In Boston, parish house facilities are being refurbished in an
urban renewal area with government cooperation and financial
assistance. Elsewhere, church groups are sponsoring housing for
the elderly under government financing. St. George's Church,
Stuyvesant Square, in New York, has established a kind of Urban
Peace Corps of the Church, whereby young adults, living together in church-owned residences, volunteer time in the evenings and on weekends for the work of the Church. Also in
New York, exploratory strategy conferences have been held
among the three dioceses that make up the metropolitan area

to consider cooperation in a sort of ecclesiastical Port of New York Authority. The Winant and Clayton Volunteers exchange college students for work in the slums of England and the United States. Other international work camps assist in city churches.

THE PLUMB LINE OF THE EUCHARIST

Still other new ventures are coming to light continually. We are living in an exciting time; the Holy Spirit is moving. As in all such times there is a danger that shots will be scattered, that there will be conflict and overlapping. We can avoid chaos if each pioneer venture is carefully tied into the ongoing life of the Church as part of the fellowship and encouraged to remain in close communication, and if all concerned bring their various ministries back to the plumb line of the Holy Communion for testing and renewal.

Be that as it may, encouraging as these signs of life may be, I continue to have anxiety about the content of the gospel, the flesh and the blood of the gospel we show forth. I hope you will excuse the subjectivity of the following. I can feel the incarnate pulse of God's love more clearly in the "slums," in close identification with those who are rejected by the culture we seek to redeem, than in the "middle-class" life of uptown and suburb, where the leaders in that culture are. In this more comfortable life, the love and passion of Christ must continually be concocted in the imagination, reached for, and laboriously described. The occasional work of the volunteer in the settlement house, the institutional approach of the social agency, be it ever so effective, the high-phrased concepts of a theology of city planning, the academic and sociological categorizing of social ills, and the like never seem to me quite as valid signs of the Kingdom as does the full sharing of another's total life, the simple footwashing of an unknown lover of God. This feeling may be sentimentality on my part. But even if it is valid, we dare not stop what seems to be the guidance of the Spirit in uncovering the reality of the presence of his passion and in seeking a more graceful framework for the movement of his love in the total structure of metropolitan life.

In this quandary are we left, still groping for the city in some blindness, weak in our allies, and so uncertain in our concepts that should we be confronted with the City, we indeed might not recognize the shimmer of its frame. Thus, in this groping we cannot afford to neglect the coming back, again and again, to the loving pattern of the Eucharist and the Eucharistic pattern of love around and about us. For here is our strength and life, our pattern and power. If the content of our faith is empty or twisted, if it is without charity, as Paul says, it is worthless.

Why am I anxious about this, you might ask. Is not the Christian faith the Christian faith when it is preached? How can it be twisted or empty? For an answer, turn to the story of Christianity in Africa. I am haunted by this story. Over the last hundred years the churches have poured in a vast volume of money, heroism, sacrifice, education, hospitals, and welfare. Men like Albert Schweitzer have put civilization behind them in order to serve the cause of Christ in Africa. Yet in the eyes of many if not most of the leaders of the new Africa, this effort has been a gigantic failure in terms of evangelism.[1]

The new Africa is not drawn to Christianity as a faith. Why? Because no matter how heroic and sincere, this missionary Christianity has been misinformed about the feelings of the Africans. In all those years, and even today on the part of devout and sensitive men, there is blindness to the deepest need of a proud people, the need for self-respect, which runs deeper than

[1] See Ram Desai, *Christianity in Africa, As Seen by the Africans* (Denver: Alan Swallow, 1962).

the sores of the lepers at Lambaréné. The result of this insensitivity of white pride may well be the loss of a continent unless, pray God, the African Christians can separate, on their own, the gospel of Christ from the actions, words, and evident feelings of many of the missionaries of Christ.

This vision of Africa haunts me, because I see the city church doing the same thing. I see time and money and heartbreak poured into the urban church over the years, and yet I fear, at the end of those years, simple but realistic men will shrug their shoulders and say, "It's too bad." These men may continue thus: "They helped our children a bit. They tried hard and were men of good will. But they did not know us really very well. And when one of us became a Christian, he seemed to leave our life. They did not live our lives and marry our daughters and speak our language. They did not understand our businesses; they never really crossed over, out of the castle of the Church, into the place we were. And frankly, we did not especially want them to, for as far as we could see they had nothing really to say to us, where we lived."

INVOLVEMENT AND IDENTIFICATION

And so we come back to the urgency of *involvement* and *identification,* as we have so often. In Africa, for the most part, the missionaries were *not* involved completely in the life of the people. They gave their blood but not their selves, it seems. They did not incarnate their beings in the blackness of Africa. They did not kneel before a black Christ. They did not contemplate marrying black. It is presumptuous to say these things, when one has never ventured out as a missionary, never made the sacrifices; I say this not to judge them but to judge myself and others who work in the modern city.

To minister to that part of the city which is poor, complete involvement and identification is, I am afraid, ultimately necessary. A quotation from William Stringfellow's *A Private and Public Faith* may clarify:

The premise of most urban church work, it seems, is that in order for the Church to minister among the poor, the Church has to be rich, that is, to have specially trained personnel, huge budgets, many facilities, rummage to distribute, and a whole battery of social services. Rather, the opposite is the case. The Church must be free to be poor in order to minister among the poor. The Church must trust the Gospel enough to come among the poor with nothing to offer the poor except the Gospel, except the power to discern and the courage to expose the Gospel as it is already mediated in the life of the poor.

When the Church has the freedom itself to be poor among the poor, it will know how to use what riches it has. When the Church has that freedom, it will know also how to minister among the rich and powerful. When the Church has that freedom, it will be a missionary people again in all the world. When the Church has that freedom to go out into the world with merely the Gospel to offer the world, then it will know how to use whatever else it has—money and talent and buildings and power in politics—as sacraments of the gift of its own life to the world, as tokens of the ministry of Christ.[2]

He does not, you see, discount the tools of the ministry of love which the Church can use, but says that they are meaningless, may be badly used, and may even stand in the way of the gospel, if first identification and the meaning of the gospel, the Kingdom, within the context of persons' particular lives is not discerned.

Involvement and identification with whatever the Church finds as she travels the world or the city—with poverty, with blackness, with Orientalness, with insanity, with leprosy, with loneliness and fear, with worldly insecurity, with imprisonment, with persecution—is the answer. How does involvement and

[2] William Stringfellow, *A Private and Public Faith* (Grand Rapids, Mich.: Wm. B. Eerdmans, 1962), pp. 80-81.

identification speak to the ministry to the aged unless it be old with the old that they may become young in Christ? And how does it work with industrial workers in factory or office, unless it be to become bored and frustrated until there be found a bored and frustrated Christ who can redeem and sanctify or leaven and change the boredom and frustration? And how does involvement and identification work with the businessman who carries the destiny of thousands in his decisions—bound, hog-tied as he is by his position from making free decisions under God—unless it be to share the captivity of the *organization*, showing the captives that captives indeed they are and that God can be worshiped in captivity, can "lead captivity captive," can free.

In the Episcopal Church, at this stage in its development, for example, this involvement means the presence of the priest, his physical presence in the context of the work to which he is pastor. This means *living* in the inner city whenever possible, if the inner city is his parish. This means being present in some way with men and women in their work, if this be his responsibility. The day will come (and I hope it will be soon) when the lay ministry will completely fulfill this function of presence. In the mind of the average person, however, the layman does not yet represent the Church except in some narrowly defined areas.

The place and time where all these ideas and relationships come true is in the Eucharist. Here is the pattern and the power. Here in the Offertory is the time and place to offer all that each life takes on in its special environment of poverty or wealth, of sickness or health. Here, as Charles Williams would say, is the time and place for an exchange—an exchange of my burden for yours, an exchange of our burdens for the light yoke of Christ, an exchange of sin and penitence for forgiveness. And in the

Consecration of the bread and wine is an exchange of our bodies for his body, of the Cross for Resurrection, of captivity for freedom, of death for life, of all else for joy.

And so wherever we are, whatever we do, we return to the touchstone of the altar to be made over into each other and into Christ. Then forth we go, layman and clergyman, from the City of God revealed in the Eucharist into the clattering city of men —ready once more to continue our search there for the City of God, however hidden it may be.

Suggested Reading

BACKGROUND

Abell, Aaron, *The Urban Impact on American Protestantism, 1865-1900.* Cambridge: Harvard University Press, 1945.

Adams, Henry, *Mont St. Michel and Chartres.* Garden City: Double-day-Anchor, 1959.

Dolling, Robert R., *Ten Years in a Portsmouth Slum.* London: S. C. Brown Langham, 1903. By an English priest—autobiographical.

Ingram, Kenneth, *Basil Jellicoe.* London: The Centenary Press, 1936. Priest of the Church of England in the slums of London at the turn of the century. Early attempts at social action for better housing.

Menzies, Lucy, *Father Wainwright.* New York: Longmans, Green, 1949. Vicar of St. Peter's, London Docks, circa 1900.

Mumford, Lewis, *The City in History.* New York: Harcourt, Brace, 1961. A major study on the subject—necessary reading.

Ruskin, John, *The Stones of Venice.* 2 vols. London: 1851. An example of early thinking about the meaning of the city, with special reference to architecture.

Troeltsch, Ernst, *The Social Teachings of the Christian Churches* (trans. Olive Wyon). New York: Harper & Bros., 1960. The definitive work on the subject originally published in 1911. German and thorough.

Weber, Max, *The City.* New York: Collier Books, 1962. Introduction contains a survey of theories of the city.

Wesley, John *Journals*. Relationship of his method to the new industrial society.

SOCIOLOGICAL STUDIES

Barnes, Roswell (ed.), *The Churches and Social Welfare*. New York: NCCCUSA, 1955. Five volumes prepared for first Conference on the Church and Social Welfare.

Conant, James, *Slums and Suburbs*. New York: McGraw-Hill, 1961. Commentary on metropolitan education in the schools.

The Exploding Metropolis, by the Editors of *Fortune* Magazine. Garden City: Doubleday-Anchor, 1958. Study of the post-World War II metropolis in the USA.

Galbraith, John Kenneth, *The Affluent Society*. Boston: Houghton Mifflin, 1958. A book that has influenced the perspective of American thinking.

Hunter, Floyd, *Community Power Structure*. Chapel Hill: University of North Carolina Press, 1953. A study of the leadership of a city of 500,000.

Jacobs, Jane, *The Death and Life of American Cities*. New York: Random House, 1961. The most provocative and most controversial book on the subject in recent years. Stresses the loss of relationship and community in modern bulldozing approach to urban renewal.

Mumford, Lewis, *The Culture of Cities*. New York: Harcourt, Brace, 1938.

Packard, Vance, *The Hidden Persuaders*. New York: David McKay, 1957.

———, *The Status-Seekers*. New York: David McKay, 1959. Advertising and status as they affect the American scene.

Reisman, David, *The Lonely Crowd*. Garden City: Doubleday, 1953. Influential study of American mass culture.

Vidich, Arthur J., and Bensman, Joseph, *Small Town in Mass Society*. Garden City: Doubleday, 1958. An exploration of social life in a community unable to determine its own existence.

Walmsley, Arthur E. (ed.), *The Church in a Society of Abundance*.

New York: Seabury, 1963. Current society and the Christian mission as viewed by nine authorities on the social sciences and on the Church.

White, Morton and Lucia, *The Intellectuals vs. the City*. Cambridge: Harvard University Press, 1963. A fascinating account of the betrayal of the American city by American intellectuals.

Whyte, William H., Jr., *The Organization Man*. New York: Simon and Schuster, 1956. Effect of large corporations on their members, especially management.

INTERCULTURAL RELATIONS
AND SPECIAL GROUPS

Arnow, Harriet, *The Dollmaker*. New York: Macmillan, 1954. A penetrating novel about the impact of the city on a rural family.

Baldwin, James, *Nobody Knows My Name*. New York: Dial, 1961. A penetrating insight into the feelings and experiences of an intelligent and sensitive Negro.

——, *The Fire Next Time*. New York: Dial, 1963. Brilliant observations on the race issue that have stirred the nation.

Bloom, Harry, *Episode in the Transvaal*. Garden City: Doubleday, 1955. A novel describing a riot in South African "location." Highly recommended by Archbishop de Blank.

Boyle, Sarah Patton, *The Desegregated Heart*. New York: Morrow, 1962. A Southern churchwoman tells of her conversion to a Christian view of race.

Campbell, Will D., *Race and Renewal of the Church*. Philadelphia: Westminster, 1962. A penetrating analysis suggesting that the answer to the racial question lies in Christian faith rather than secular facts.

——, *We Are a Third Race*. Cincinnati: Forward Movement Publications, 1962. A condensation in pamphlet form of *Race and Renewal of the Church*.

Drake, St. Clair and Cayton, Horace, *Black Metropolis*. New York: Harcourt, Brace, 1945. Sociological study of Negro section of Chicago.

Gross, Alfred A., *Strangers in Our Midst*. Washington, D.C.: Public
Affairs Press, 1962. A sound introduction to the problems of
the homosexual in our society.

Handlin, Oscar, *The Newcomers: Negroes and Puerto Ricans in a
Changing Metropolis*. Cambridge: Harvard University Press,
1959.

Harrington, Michael, *The Other American, Poverty in the United
States*. New York: Macmillan, 1962. A writer for *The Catholic
Worker* comments with clarity and passion on the America many
never see.

Huddleston, Trevor, *Naught for Your Comfort*. Garden City: Doubleday, 1956. The dilemma of the Church in South Africa.

Hughes, Langston, *The Ways of White Folks*. New York: Alfred A.
Knopf, 1947. A series of subtle short stories by a leading Negro
author.

————, and De Carvara, Roy, *The Sweet Flypaper of Life*. New
York: Simon and Schuster, 1955. Delightful photographic essay
on life in Harlem.

Myrdal, Gunnar, *The American Dilemma*. New York: Harper & Bros.,
1944. The classic study of race-relations in USA.

Pettigrew, Thomas F. and Campbell, Ernest Q., *Christians in Racial
Crisis*. Washington, D.C.: Public Affairs Press, 1959. A study of
Little Rock's ministry.

Saenger, Gerhart, *The Social Psychology of Prejudice*. New York:
Harper & Bros., 1953.

Smith, Lillian, *Killers of the Dream*. New York: Norton, 1949. A profound analysis of the roots of the race problem in USA.

Spark, Muriel, *Memento Mori*. Philadelphia: Lippincott, 1928. Short
novel containing remarkable insight on the aged.

Wakefield, Dan, *Island in the City*. Cambridge, Mass.: Houghton
Mifflin, 1959. Spanish Harlem, Puerto Rican ghetto in New York.

GENERAL WORKS ON THE URBAN CHURCH

Bibliography for the Urban Church. Pamphlet prepared by Department of Church Planning and Research of the Protestant Council of the City of New York. Compiled by Carolyn J. Odell.

Chapin, T. S., *The Protestant Church in an Urban Environment in Cities and Society*. Glencoe, Ill.: Free Press, 1951. A detailed discussion of sociological and religious factors as they affect the city church.

Chélini, Jean, *La Ville et L'Eglise*. Les Editions du Cerf, 29 boulevard Latour-Maubourg, Paris 7, 1958. French study of urban religious sociology. Contains rather complete bibliography of Continental works on the subject.

Greeley, Andrew M., *The Church and the Suburbs*. New York: Sheed & Ward, 1959. Roman Catholic problems are parallel to ours.

Kloetzli, Walter, *The Church and the Urban Challenge*. Philadelphia: Muhlenberg, 1961. Addresses on urban problems and the Church's response (touched lightly).

Kloetzli, Walter and Hillman, Arthur, *Urban Church Planning*. Philadelphia: Muhlenberg, 1958. Includes planning on the administrative level above the parish.

Leiffer, Murray, *The Effective City Church*. New York, Board of Missions, Methodist Church, 1954. A well rounded book on parish work in the city.

Miller, Kenneth, *Man and God in the City*. New York: Friendship Press, 1954. An early book from the Protestant view on the city church.

Neusse and Harte, *The Sociology of the Parish*. Milwaukee: Bruce, 1950. A treatment of the subject from a Roman Catholic viewpoint.

The Task of the Church in Relation to Industry. Church Information Office, Church House, Westminster, SW 1, England. Outlines basic philosophy of Edward Wickham and the Industrial Missions of England. See also publications of the *Detroit Industrial Mission*.

Viewpoints, Editors John Coburn and Norman Pittenger. New York: Seabury, 1959. Especially Chapter 17 by Paul Moore, Jr., which contains survey of urban work in the Episcopal Church.

Webber, George W., *God's Colony in Man's World*. Nashville: Abingdon, 1960. Essays on the Church by a founder of the East Harlem Protestant Parish.

Wickham, E. R., *Church and People in an Industrial City*. London: Lutterworth, 1957. A history of the Church in Sheffield, England.

Winter, Gibson, *New Creation as Metropolis*. New York: Macmillan, 1963.

————, *The Suburban Captivity of the Churches*. Garden City: Doubleday, 1961. Most effective study yet to appear on the contemporary problem. Accurate and profound. Thin on solutions.

LITURGICAL AND THEOLOGICAL

Augustine, *City of God*. A theological classic.

Ayres, Francis O., *The Ministry of the Laity*. Philadelphia: Westminster, 1962.

Hebert, A. G., *Liturgy and Society*. London: S.P.C.K., 1937. An early classic of the liturgical movement.

Shands, Alfred Rives, *The Liturgical Movement and the Local Church*. London: SCM Press, 1959. An enthusiastic account of the way in which the local church begins to study its neighbors, looking towards a liturgical strategy for the parish.

Southcott, Ernest W., *Receive This Child*. London: Mowbray, 1955. Baptism in the urban parish.

Stringfellow, William, *A Private and Public Faith*. Grand Rapids, Mich.: Wm. B. Eerdmans, 1962. Biting theological essays relevant to urban America.

Williams, Charles, *The Image of the City*. New York: Oxford University Press, 1958. A fresh theology of the Kingdom.

THE URBAN CHURCH AT WORK

Allan, Tom, *The Face of My Parish*. New York: Harper & Bros., 1957. A city parish in contemporary England.

Bishop, Claire Huchet, *France Alive*. New York: Farrar-Straus, 1947. Survey of the awakening of the Church in France after the war.

Darling, Edward M., *Highways, Hedges, and Factories*. Toronto: Longmans, Green, 1957.

de Blank, Joost, *The Parish in Action*. London: Longmans, Green,

1954. Recognizing the inadequacy of time-honored methods, the author suggests new ways for the parish to fulfill its responsibility to those outside "the worshiping community."

Ehle, John, *Shepherd of the Streets*. New York: Morrow, 1960. The story of the Rev. James Gusweller and his fight for better housing among Puerto Ricans in New York.

Fichter, Joseph H., S.J., *Social Relations in the Urban Parish*. Chicago: University of Chicago Press, 1954. A Roman Catholic study of this subject.

Kenrick, Bruce, *Come Out the Wilderness*. New York: Harper & Row, 1962. The story of the East Harlem Protestant Parish.

Kloetzli, Walter, *The City Church, Death or Renewal*. Philadelphia: Muhlenberg, 1961. Studies in some depth of eight Lutheran urban parishes.

Kothen, Robert, *The Priest and the Proletariat*. New York: Sheed & Ward, 1948. The Church's separation from the worker.

Lee, Robert (ed.), *Cities and Churches*. Philadelphia: Westminster, 1962. Anthology of articles on the urban church in America.

Lloyd, Roger, *An Adventure in Discipleship*. London: Longmans, Green, 1955. Developing the Christian "cell."

Loew, Jacques, *Mission to the Poorest*. New York: Sheed & Ward, 1950. The spiritual dynamic of a ministry to the very poor. Pere Loew works in Marseilles.

Michonneau, Abbe George, *Revolution in a City Parish*. Westminster, Md.: Newman, 1950. A book which had a great impact on parish philosophy over the last decade.

Musselman, G. Paul, *The Church on the Urban Frontier*. New York: Seabury, 1960. Urban study by an Episcopalian. Full of immensely useful facts and insights.

Myers, C. Kilmer, *Light the Dark Streets*. New York: Seabury, 1957. Ministry to gangs on New York Lower East Side.

Priest-Workman in England. London: S.P.C.K., 1951. An autobiographical account by an Anglican priest, his attempt to follow the techniques of the French Worker-Priests.

Sanderson, Ross, *The Church Serves the Changing City*. New York: Harper & Bros., 1955. Case histories of several urban parishes in the U.S.A.—illustrated. Includes article on Grace Church, Jersey City.

Southcott, Ernest W., *The Parish Comes Alive*. New York: Morehouse-Barlow, 1956. New techniques in urban ministry, especially the House Church and parish Eucharist.

Wilson, H. A., *Haggerston Year, Jig-saw, Haggerston Sermons*, etc. London: Mowbray, 1935-1950. Short stories from the life of a London priest. Romantic, but valid.

PERIODICALS

The Catholic Worker, Editor, Dorothy Day. 175 Chrystie St., New York, New York.

The City Church, published by the Department of the Urban Church, National Council of the Churches of Christ, USA, 475 Riverside Drive, New York.

New City, Man in Metropolis, a Christian Response, published by the Roman Catholic Council on Working Life. Subscription office, 21 W. Superior Street, Chicago 10, Illinois.

Appendix A

Statement of Aims and Principles of Urban Mission Priests, 1953

The Urban Mission Priests is a group of more than fifty clergy who are involved or keenly interested in the work of the Church in the so-called blighted areas of the metropolitan centers.

PURPOSE

1. To promote the Church in these areas.
2. To bring into the Church the residents of these areas.
3. To raise up leadership within the Church to concern itself with the great social issues of the day, a leadership strengthened by members whose daily lives are affected by economic and social injustice or race discrimination.

TENTATIVE PRINCIPLES OF THE URBAN MISSION PRIESTS

1. A *Group Ministry* is almost essential in a "depressed" area, because of the great number of pastoral problems which exist there and the need for a small nucleus around which to build the community of the parish.

2. There must be a place where all who come will always find a warm welcome, a feeling of love and acceptance, which need has been met in some places by the "open rectory."
3. *Evangelism* can often be furthered by participation in activity seemingly quite unrelated to the spiritual life, such as recreation and social action.
4. *Our ministry must be to the total life of the individual and to the whole neighborhood.*
5. *Paternalism* must be guarded against, when the parish is receiving outside financial assistance, by close association of clergy, staff, and people in their way of life; dependency must be guarded against by developing a sense of financial responsibility in the parish itself.
6. *The Altar* is the center of the community, the place to which people are led, the place from which they go forth to carry Christ into the world.
7. The *liturgical life* of the parish must come alive and be the means of expressing the redemptive activity in which the community is involved.
8. All *false barriers* of race, national origin, and economic status must be broken through, that all may be joined, one to the other, in Christian love.
9. The Christian community should express its concern for social justice through a *social action* program, arising from the parish experience, and expressed by laymen as well as clergy.
10. The combination of *Catholic* spiritual power and *Protestant* freedom and democratic polity, which is the heritage of the *Episcopal Church,* gives her a peculiar responsibility in this field.

RESULTS OF URBAN MISSION PRIESTS GROUP

1. Monthly meetings for discussion and working out of problems have been held for almost three years.
2. Summer training programs for college, graduate, and seminary students have been conducted.

3. Aid has been given to Diocesan authorities in clergy placement.
4. Urban Mission Priests have been instrumental in the initiating and planning of several new works in this field.
5. Urban Mission Priests groups have been started in Boston and Philadelphia.
6. An Urban Laymen's Group has been meeting for eight months to complement the efforts of the Priests.
7. Seminary Associates of the Urban Priests have been started in several seminaries to educate and to stimulate vocations to this work.
8. The Urban Mission Priests have taken a public stand on some of the social issues within and without the Church.
9. Indirect influence.

CONCLUSION

The money to do the work is in the possession of members of the Episcopal Church; vocations to the work are increasing; but there are thousands of souls to reach.

We invite all Christians to help us in whatever way they can in fulfilling our aims.

We ask to be remembered in your prayers.

Interim Statement of the Aims and Purposes of the Urban Laymen's Group

The Urban Laymen's Group is associated with the Urban Mission Priests for the purpose of cooperating with and assisting them in carrying out the work of the Church in depressed areas of metropolitan centers. As a cooperating group, our purposes are essentially the same as those of the Urban Mission Priests:

1. To promote the Church in these areas.
2. To bring into the Church the residents of these areas.

3. To raise up leadership within the Church which will concern itself with the great social issues of the day, a leadership strengthened by members whose daily lives are affected by economic and social injustice or race discrimination.

On the operating level (the parish) the Urban Laymen's Group is a group of dedicated laymen who associate themselves with the parish priest to discover ways and means of carrying out the basic concepts indicated in the purposes listed above. The Urban Laymen's Group in its larger sense is a clearing house for ideas and problems of the individual parish.

Serious consideration of the above statements leads us to realize our inadequacy and consequent need for God's help. As this help is provided by the sacraments of the Church, we pledge ourselves to a regular attendance at the Holy Communion, and to a regular schedule of daily prayer. By these we may prepare ourselves to carry out our beliefs into every area of our lives:

1. In the Parish
    Demonstrating to all the on-going life of the Church.
    Showing a love and acceptance of all people.
2. In our daily lives
    In our witness to the reality of God's love and concern for all men.
    In our Christian response to the needs and problems of others.
    In the true spirit of Evangelism, whereby we see God in every man.

We believe that these principles take practical form when we cooperate with the parish priest in ways listed below:

1. Forming a Parish Social Action group.
    Studying legislation, both national and state, which would affect social problems or minority groups.
    Conducting and participating in study groups (in the Parish House or in homes) on religious questions and social problems.

2. Making hospital visits and house visits to the sick.
   Making parish calls.
   Planning and supervising youth work.
3. Assisting at Coffee Hours.
   Supervising "open rectory."
   And in such other ways as may come out through a discussion of this paper or through individual parish experience.

We believe that the lay responsibility extends throughout the entire fabric of the Church. We look to our parish priests for spiritual leadership and guidance, but recognize that the ultimate goal is full participation by the laity on all levels of activity.

Appendix B

Tentative Proposal for Self-Study of Christ Church Cathedral to Determine Our Future Vocation

The clergy and vestry submitted this outline to the various parish organizations for their comment. The reasons for a self-study which they cited were these: the structure of our society is changing more quickly today than ever before in history, and there are special factors in the downtown situation.

The positive factors to which they referred were these: (1) our church is closer to the heart of the city and its problems, (2) it is easier to have a cross-section of people here, and (3) we have a vital vocation of evangelism, witness, prophecy, and healing; there is a deep *need* for us in the city. Negative factors in their downtown situation were the low percentage of downtown residents, the inconvenience of attending a downtown church, the spreading out of the congregation over a larger area, and the tendency to impersonality or lack of neighborliness.

The roles of the laymen as ministers and of the clergy, who cannot do all that should be done, were cited. The additional question raised was that of the role of the parish. Should it be a close-knit, very organized single community? or should it be several communities?

There is a need for joint study of laymen, who know their situation and needs, and of clergy, who have theological and technical training. Inasmuch as the parish is a joint effort, the job of the parish should be a joint decision. Furthermore, such a study process should involve as many people as possible, for those who participate will be converted to an enthusiastic course of action.

PLAN OF A SMALL GROUP SELF-STUDY

A. In proposing a plan for small group study in twelve sessions, the preliminary step obviously would be to sign up participants. Then the division of the groups could be done by several methods or categories: men, women, couples, mixed, young people, or geographical areas.

B. The subjects suggested for the first five study meetings were these: (1) the need for self-study and bibilical exploration of the subject, (2) Christ's purpose for a father, a wife, a businessman—or anyone, (3) the church's present purpose (4) the layman's role as minister, and (5) the church's method in carrying out its purpose.

C. In the following three meetings the findings from preceding sessions were to be related to answering three questions. What is the role of a parish in the Episcopal Church? What is the role of a downtown parish and does a church belong in the city? What is the role of Christ Church Cathedral here and now?

D. For the last four sessions the groups were to be re-formed according to special interests. They would consider the following: evangelism, worship and music, public relations, social relations, education, pastoral work, the Cathedral, and finance.

Group meetings were to last for just one hour, and the first six or seven sessions were to be held during Lent. Each group would have a lay discussion leader and a recorder who would record the findings of each group and hand them in weekly. The leaders would meet periodically with the clergy. At the conclusion of the twelve sessions, a coordinating group would go over the material and make a report for the consideration of the parish as a whole to plan future action.

Having given in detail the plan to be considered, the clergy and vestry concluded with this statement: "This is a real pioneering job and as far as we know has never been attempted in this fashion. It is an urgent job, but we must be ready to take plenty of time, so that it will be thoughtfully and carefully done."

The first two phases of the proposed plan as it was carried out in later months are hereafter illustrated:

PHASE I: SAMPLE
OF OUTLINE FOR ONE SESSION

BIBLE PASSAGES

On reading through these passages keep two thoughts in your mind:—

(1) What is the meaning of the passage?
(2) What do you feel it is saying to you?

I Corinthians 12: 13, 26, 27

". . . By one Spirit are we all baptized into one Body, whether we be Jews or Gentiles, whether we be slave or free; and have been made to drink into one Spirit. . . . Whether one member suffer, all members suffer with it; or one member be honored, all the members rejoice with it. Now you are the Body of Christ and members of it individually."

Commentary: Part of the correspondence to the Church at Corinth. I Corinthians contains vast and important summaries of St. Paul's understanding of the Christian Faith. Speaking here of the nature of the Church. (This chapter immediately precedes the well known 13th Chapter, ". . . Faith, Hope, Charity, these three" . . .) Probably prior to 57 A.D.

St. John 20: 19-21

". . . The same day at evening, being the first day of the week, when the doors were shut where the disciples were assembled for fear of the Jews, came Jesus and stood in the midst, and saith unto them, 'Peace be unto you.' And when He had so said, He showed unto them His hands and His side. Then were the disciples glad when they saw the Lord. Then said Jesus to them again, 'Peace be unto you; as my Father hath sent Me, even so, send I you.' "

Commentary: The time is Easter night. One of the Appearances of the Risen Lord to the Twelve Apostles.

QUESTIONS TO BE DISCUSSED

What is the work of The Church?
How does The Church suffer?
Whom ought The Church to reach?

COLLECTS

These should be used prior to the meeting.

Blessed Lord, who hast caused all holy Scriptures to be written for our learning; Grant that we may in such wise hear them, read, mark, learn, and inwardly digest them, that by patience and comfort of thy holy Word, we may embrace, and ever hold fast, the blessed hope of everlasting life, which thou hast given us in our Saviour Jesus Christ. Amen.

O God, Holy Ghost, Sanctified of the faithful, visit, we pray thee, our Parish with thy love and favour; enlighten our minds more and more with the light of the everlasting Gospel; graft in our hearts a love of the truth; increase in us true religion; nourish us with all goodness; and of thy great mercy keep us in the same, O blessed Spirit, whom, with the Father and the Son together, we worship and glorify as one God, world without end. Amen.

Close Session with *Our Father* and the *Grace*.

PHASE II: GENERAL PLAN

INTRODUCTION:

About 200 members of our parish took part in the Bible Study Groups during Lent and discussed the reasons for our parish and its purpose in general. Many different ideas came out of the experience and most of us are still rather nebulous in our thinking. This is good! Now, having plowed the ground of our thinking, we are ready to sow the seeds and work toward the harvest.

The second phase of our program will be planning the practical application of the ideas and insights we gained in the Bible study.

Committees are to be formed to study the following aspects of our parish life. (The subtitles are merely suggestions of the kinds of thing each committee will be working on.)

EVANGELISM:

(a) House calling on newcomers; (b) Hospitality; (c) Program and worship as it is related to newcomers; (d) New groups that might be formed to draw in new people (i.e., businessmen, secretaries, hobby groups); (e) How to integrate new members into the life of the parish; and (f) Ushers; volunteer receptionists.

WORSHIP:

(a) Scheduled Services—Type and time of services—Effect on members; (b) Acoustics; (c) Prayer groups; (d) Special Services; (e) Noonday Services; and (f) Quiet Days.

PUBLIC RELATIONS:

(a) Mass Communications; (b) Newspapers; (c) Signs, Fliers, etc.; (d) Hotels; (e) Use of Cathedral by outside groups; and (f) Ushers, Hospitality Committee, Volunteer Receptionists also operate under this heading.

SOCIAL RELATIONS:

(a) Christian citizenship; (b) Christian Social Welfare (transients, youth, the aging, etc.); and (c) Social Action.

CHRISTIAN EDUCATION:

(a) Church School; (b) All adult education; (c) Education for Christian living; (d) Library and tracts; and (e) Education outside parish membership, as in Forums.